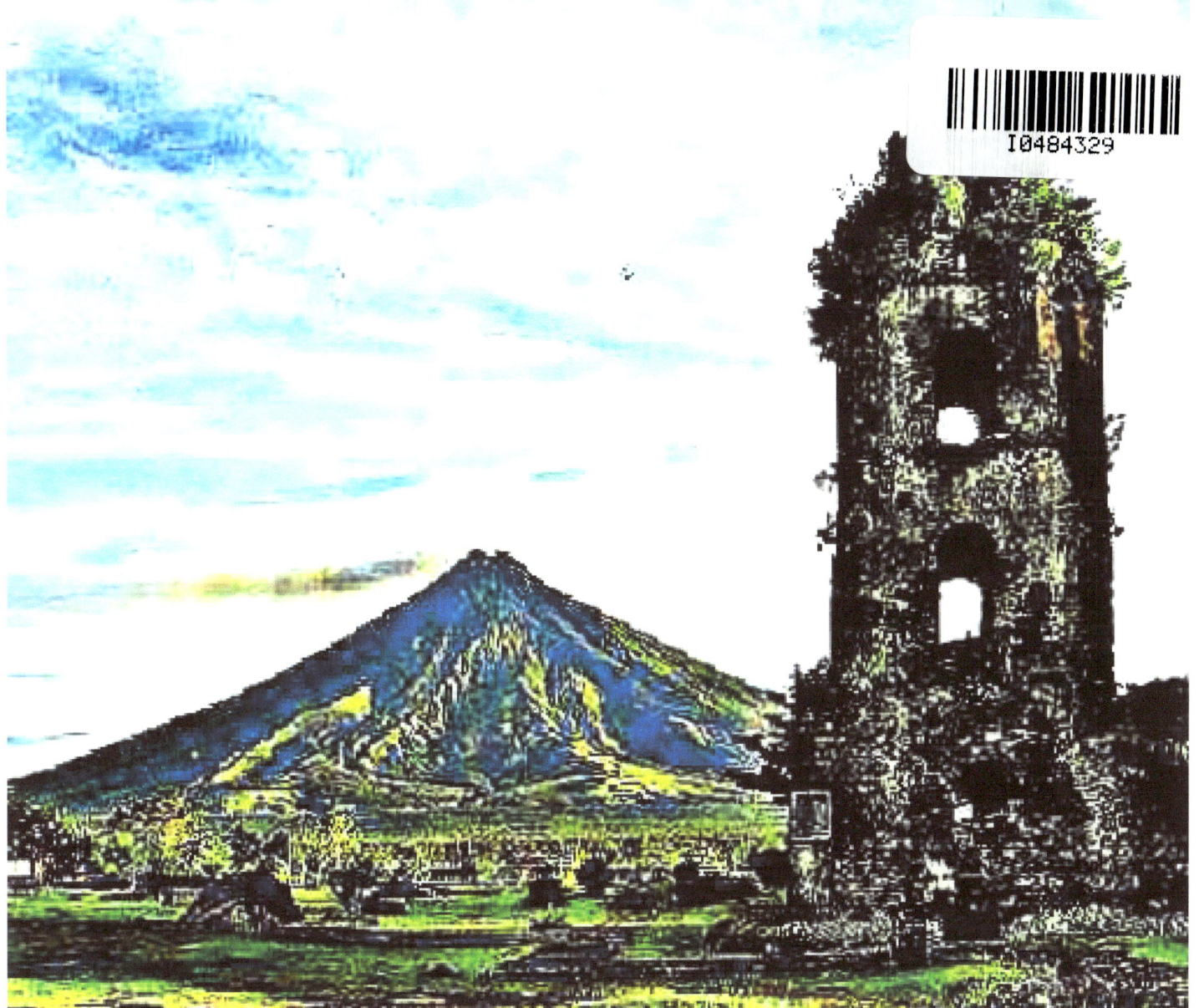

Mayon Volcano, computer-generated.

WELCOME! We hope you enjoy this Fave Art-6 collection of my favorite art works. Most art works are copied from the internet, posters, pictures and books. They are computer-generated and enhanced digitally. You may display this book as coffee table book in your living room, as conversation piece. You may give this as gift . You may cut out and frame each page. Each art work is 8.5x11 inches and suitable for framing, and then wall decors. Most art works are done by me, the self-publisher, via computer-generated enhancement. Some paintings are courtesy of my friends, such as Hermes Alegre, Khristina Reed Manansala and Ronna Manansala.

The ISBN Code Numbers of this book are:
ISBN-13: 978- 1502979193 & ISBN-10: 1502979195
Printed in USA.
Free to copy by anybody. Why copy? Just buy the book.
My other books list can be accessed at:
http://tinyurl.com/mj76ccq and http://jobelizes.webs.com.
My contact email is job_elizes@yahoo.com. Thanks

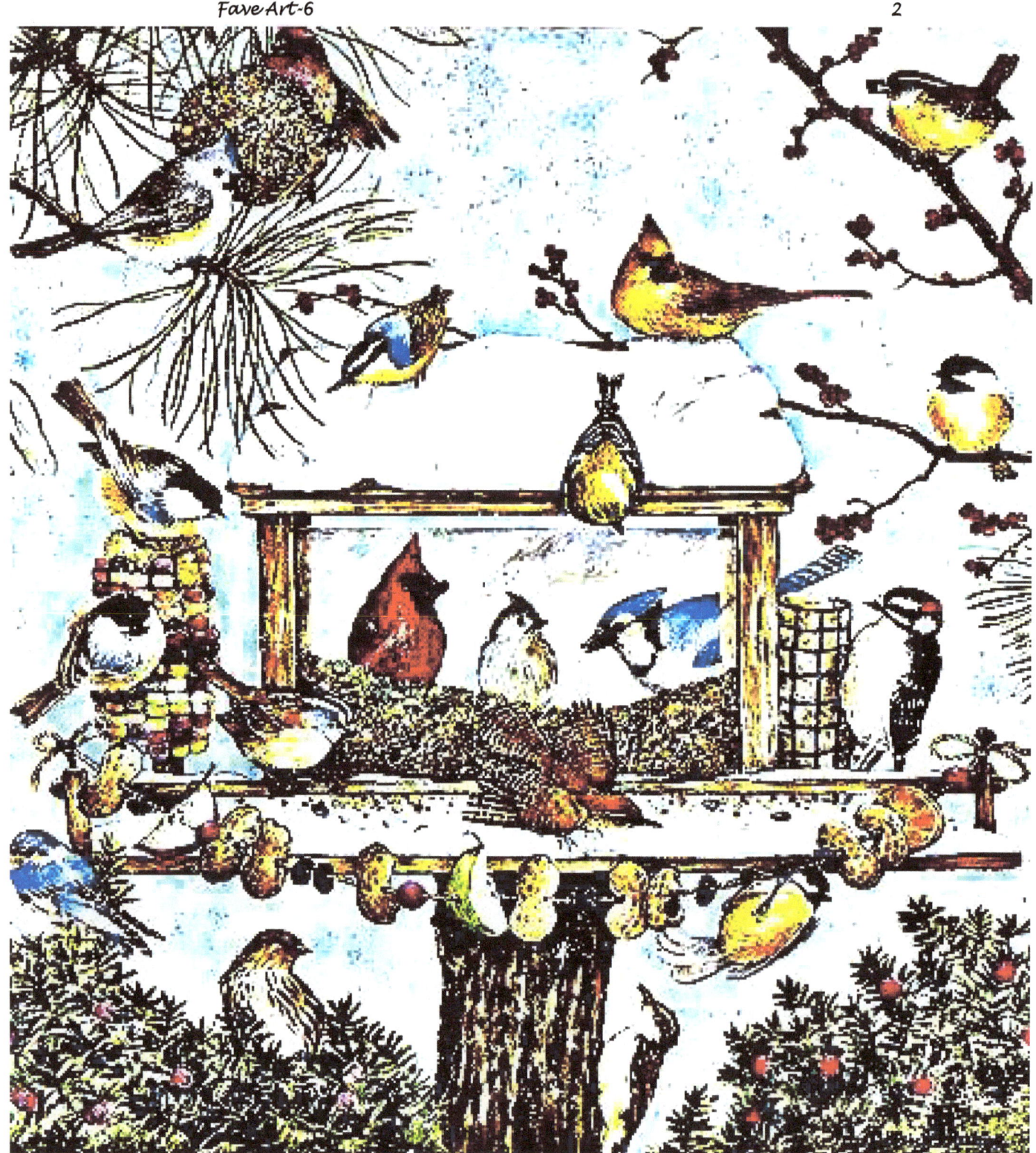

WELCOME! We hope you enjoy this Fave Art-6 collection of my favorite art works. Most art works are copied from the internet, posters, pictures and books. They are manipulated and enhanced digitally. You may display this book as coffee table book in your living room, as conversation piece. You may give this as gift . You may cut out and frame each page. Each art work is 8.5x11 inches and suitable for framing, and then wall decors. Most art works are done by me, the self-publisher, via computer-generated enhancement. Some artworks are courtesy of my friend-artists. Free to copy by anybody. Why copy when you can buy cheaply. My other books list can be accessed at: http://tinyurl.com/mj76ccq and http://jobelizes.webs.com. My contact email is job_elizes@yahoo.com. Thanks

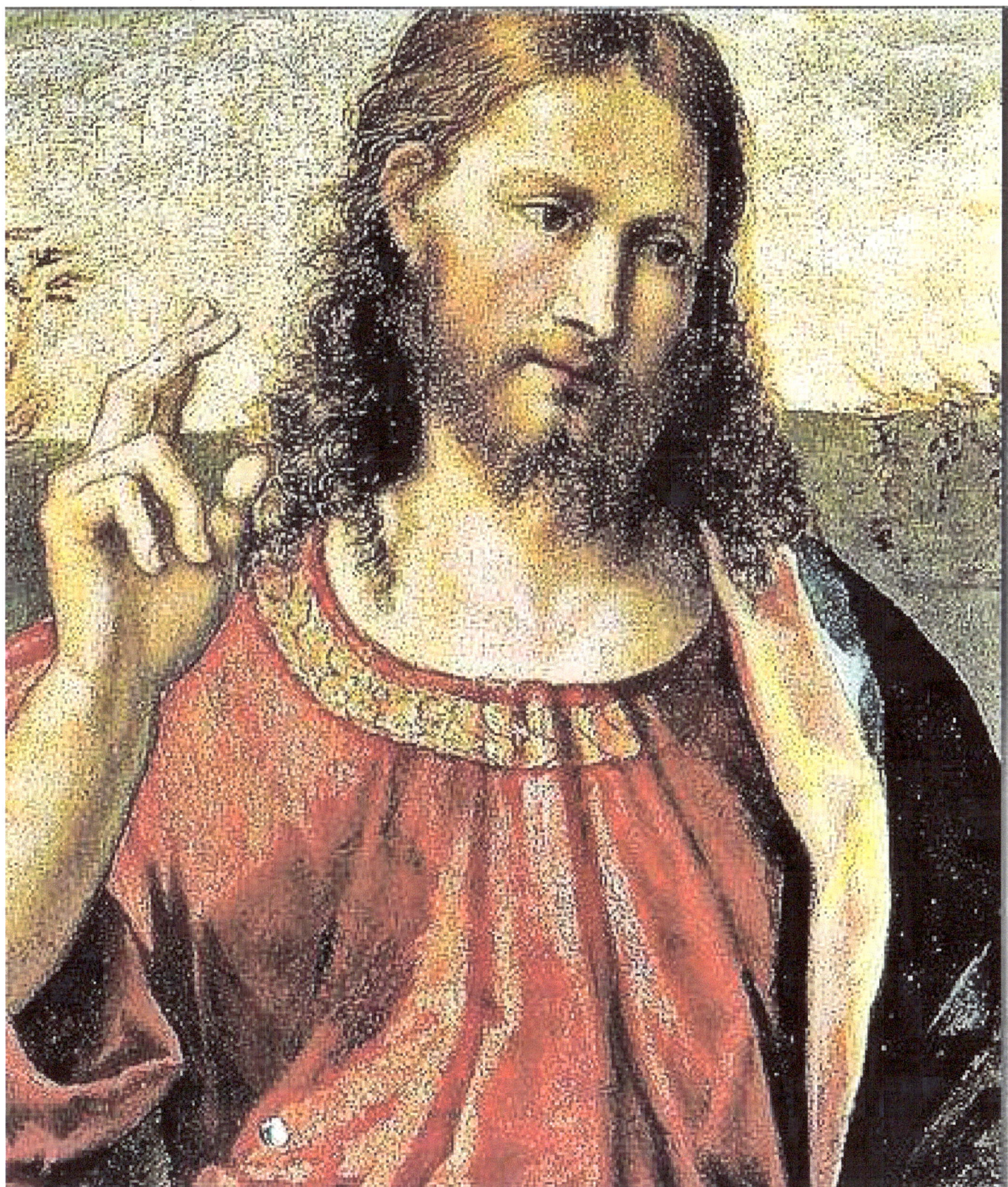

WELCOME! We hope you enjoy this Fave Art-6 collection of my favorite art works. Most art works are copied from the internet, posters, pictures and books. They are manipulated and enhanced digitally. You may display this book as coffee table book in your living room, as conversation piece. You may give this as gift . They are enhanced digitally. You may cut out and frame each page. Each art work is 8.5x11 inches and suitable for framing, and then wall decors. Most art works are done by me, the self-publisher, via computer enhancement. Some are contributed by my friend-artists. My booklist can be accessed at: http://tinyurl.com/mj76ccq and http://jobelizes.webs.com. My contact email is job_elizes@yahoo.com. Thanks

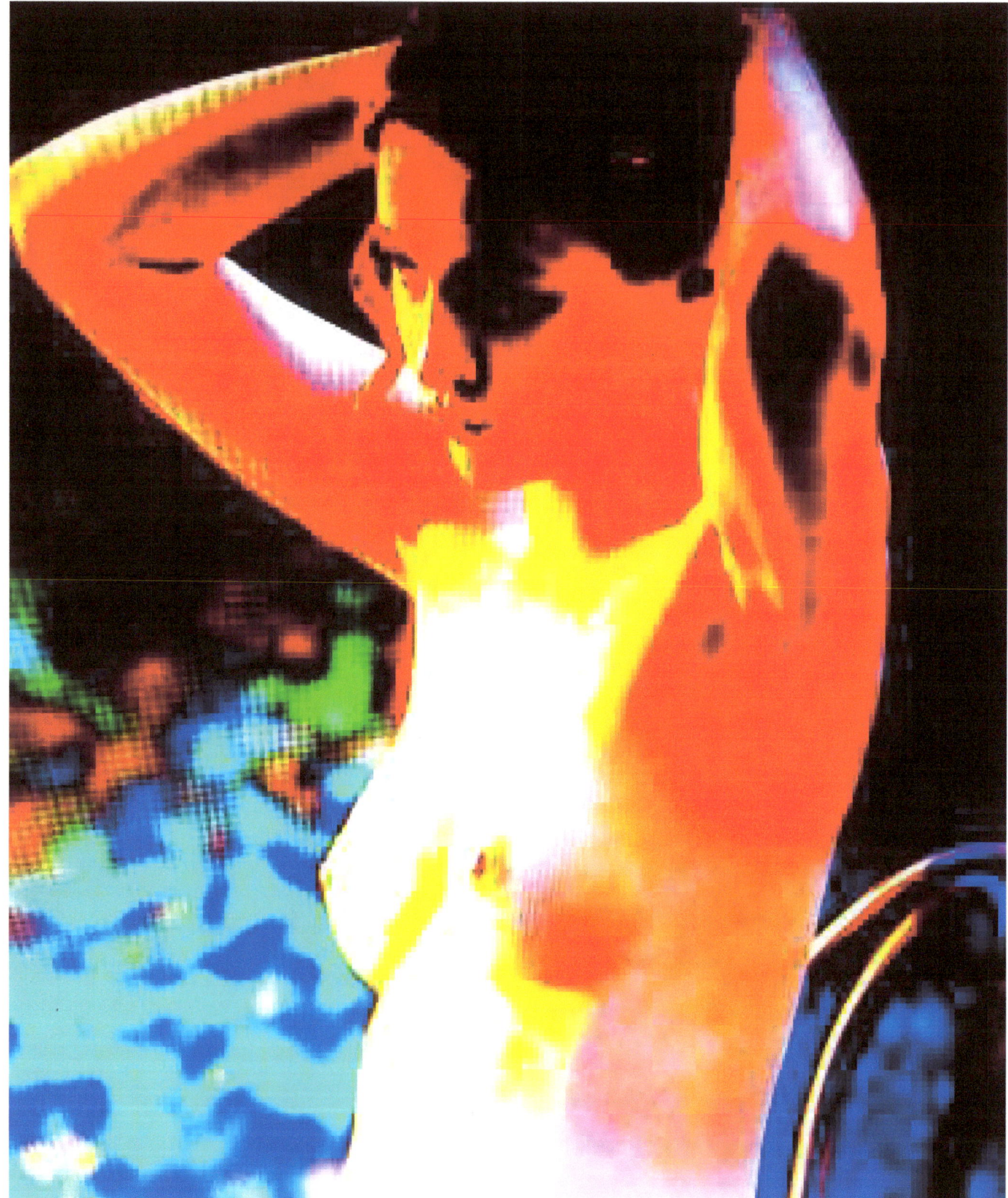

WELCOME! We hope you enjoy this Fave Art-6 collection of my favorite art works. Most art works are copied from the internet, posters, pictures and books. They are manipulated and enhanced digitally. You may display this book as coffee table book in your living room, as conversation piece. You may give this as gift . They are enhanced digitally. You may cut out and frame each page. Each art work is 8.5x11 inches and suitable for framing, and then wall decors. Most art works are done by me, the self-publisher, via computer enhancement. Some are contributed by my friend-artists. My other books list can be accessed at: http://tinyurl.com/mj76ccq and http://jobelizes.webs.com. My contact email is job_elizes@yahoo.com. Thanks

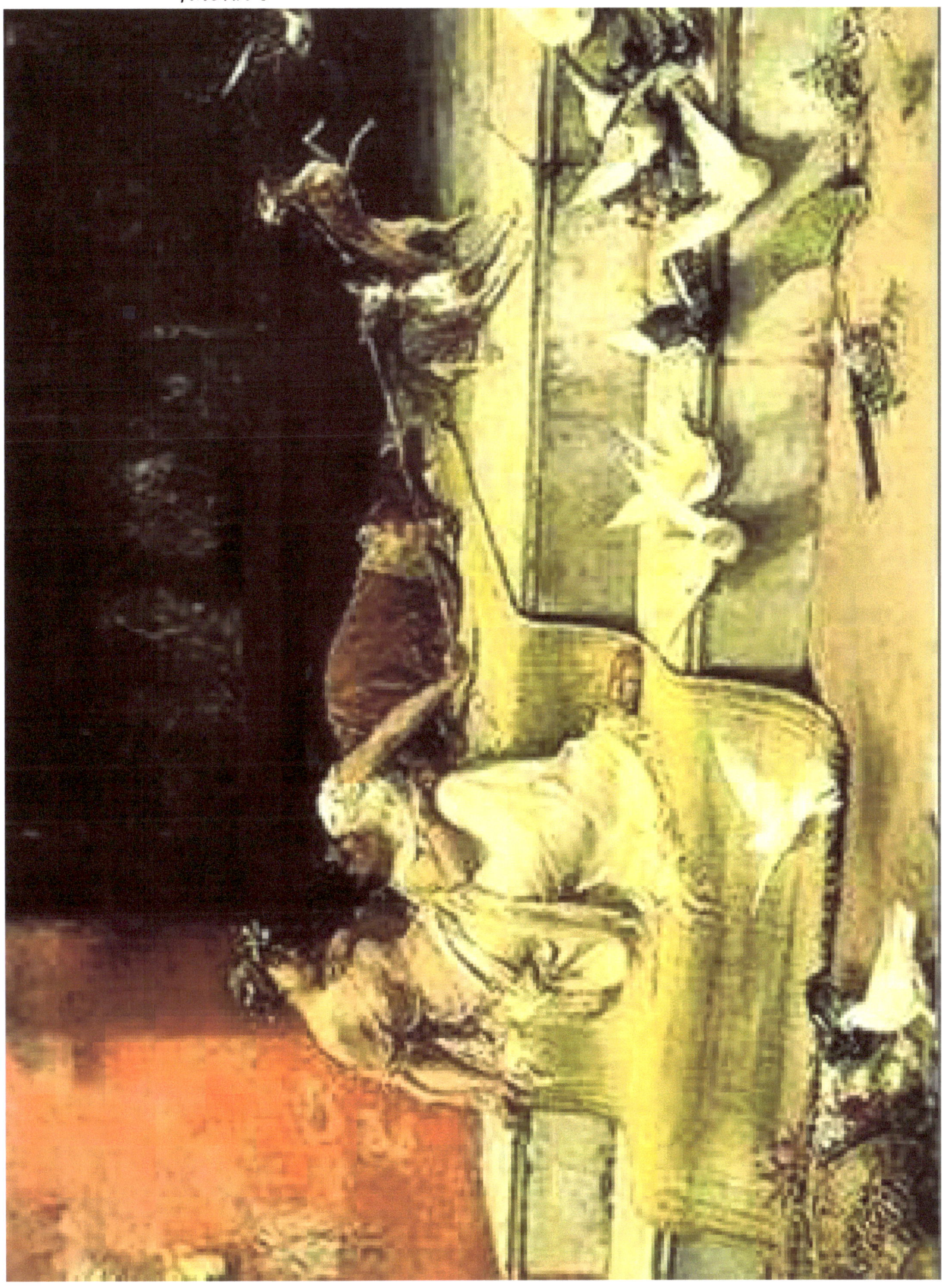

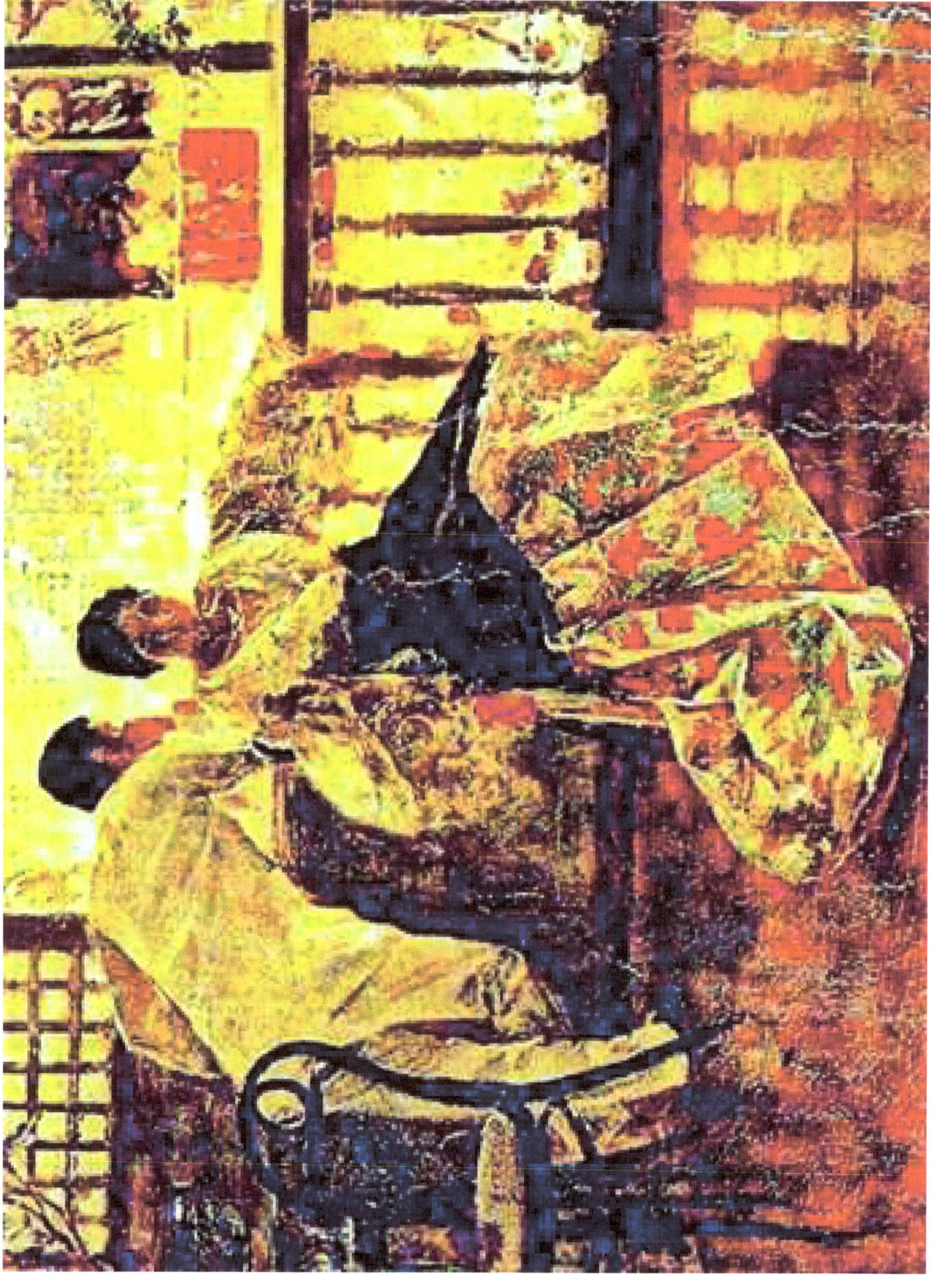

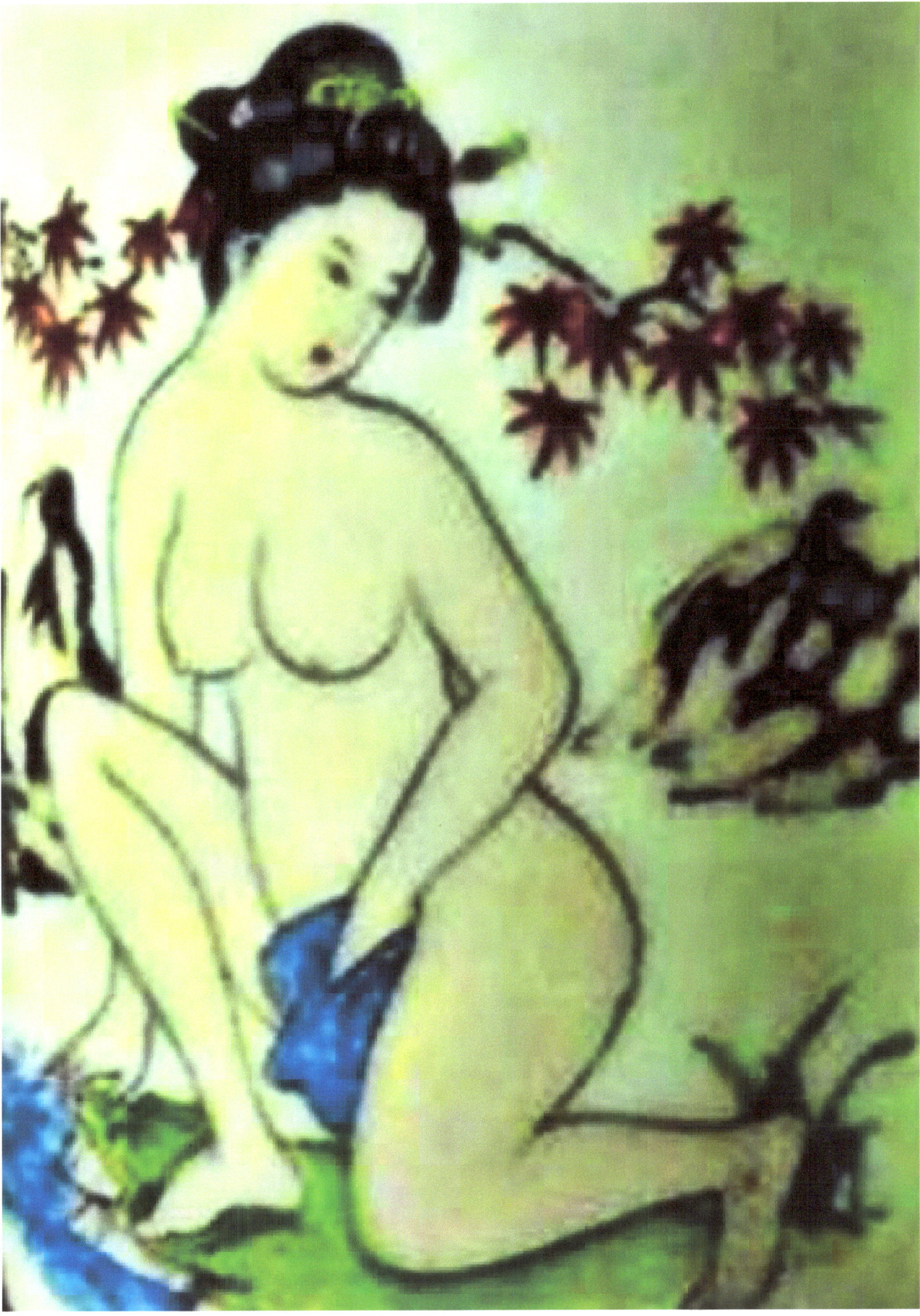

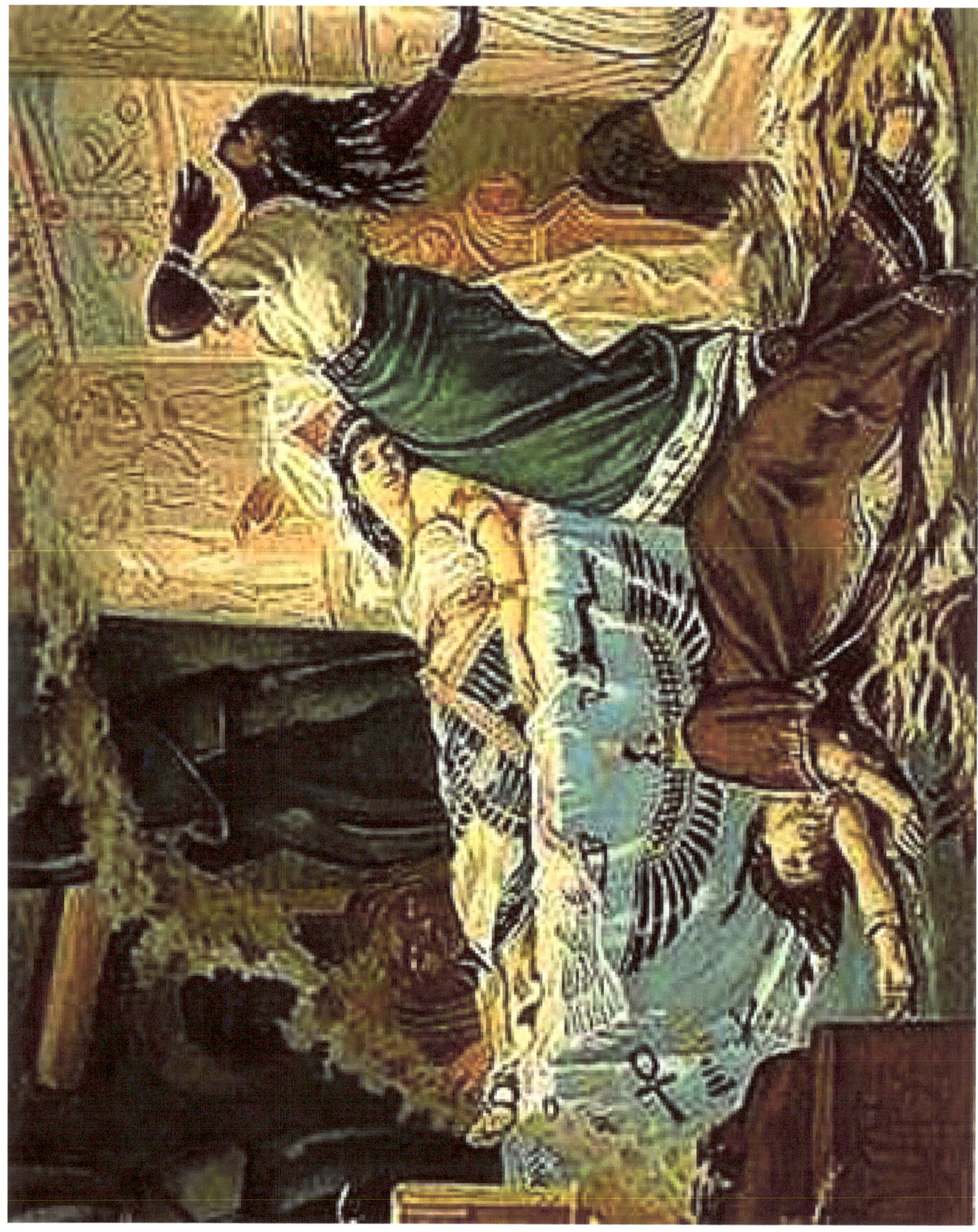

The Nude Sculpture & Butt Sculpture pieces on next 2 pages are photos of Art Works done by
National Artist NAPOLEON ABUEVA of UP. Photos taken at his Museum-home in Q.C.

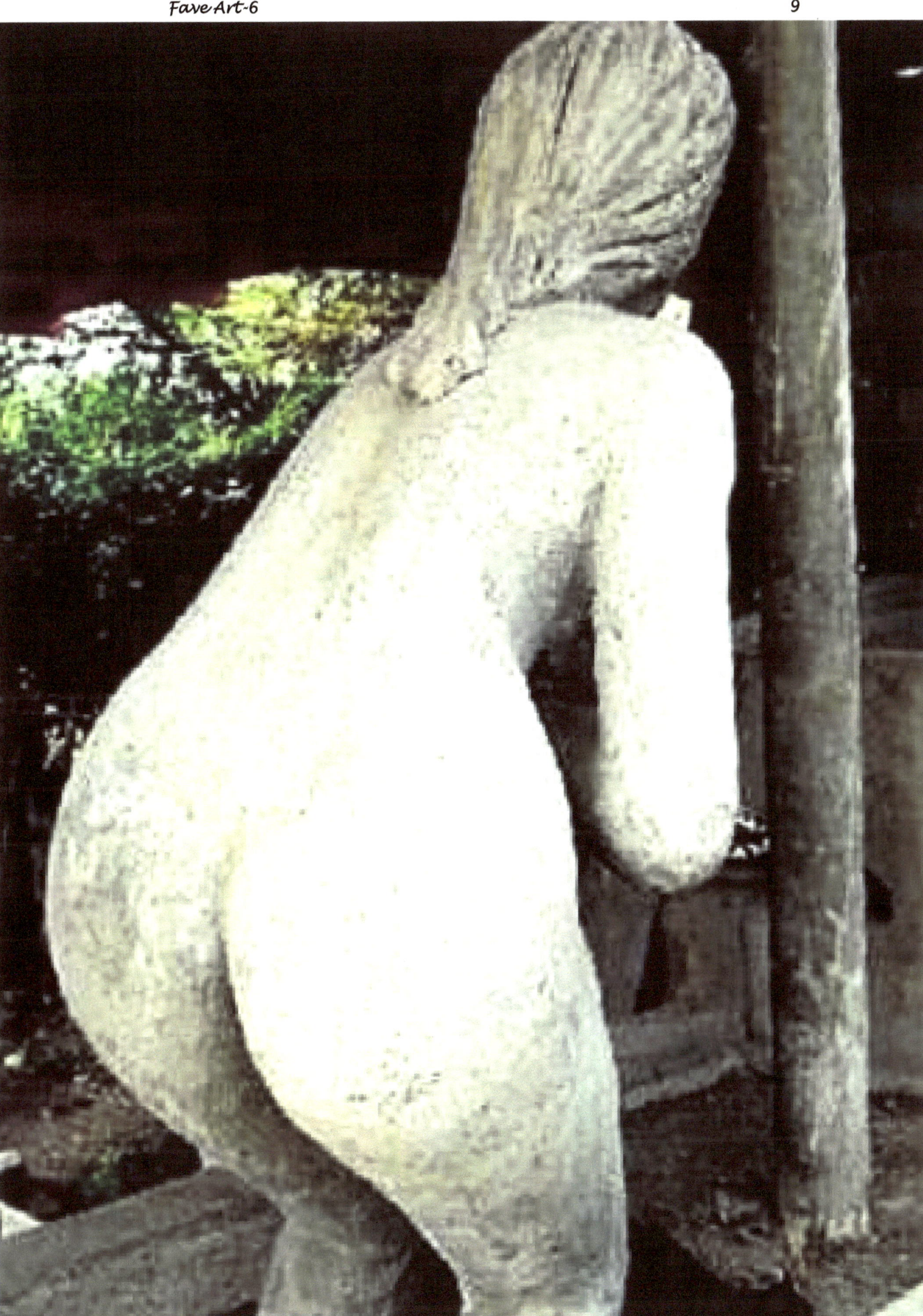

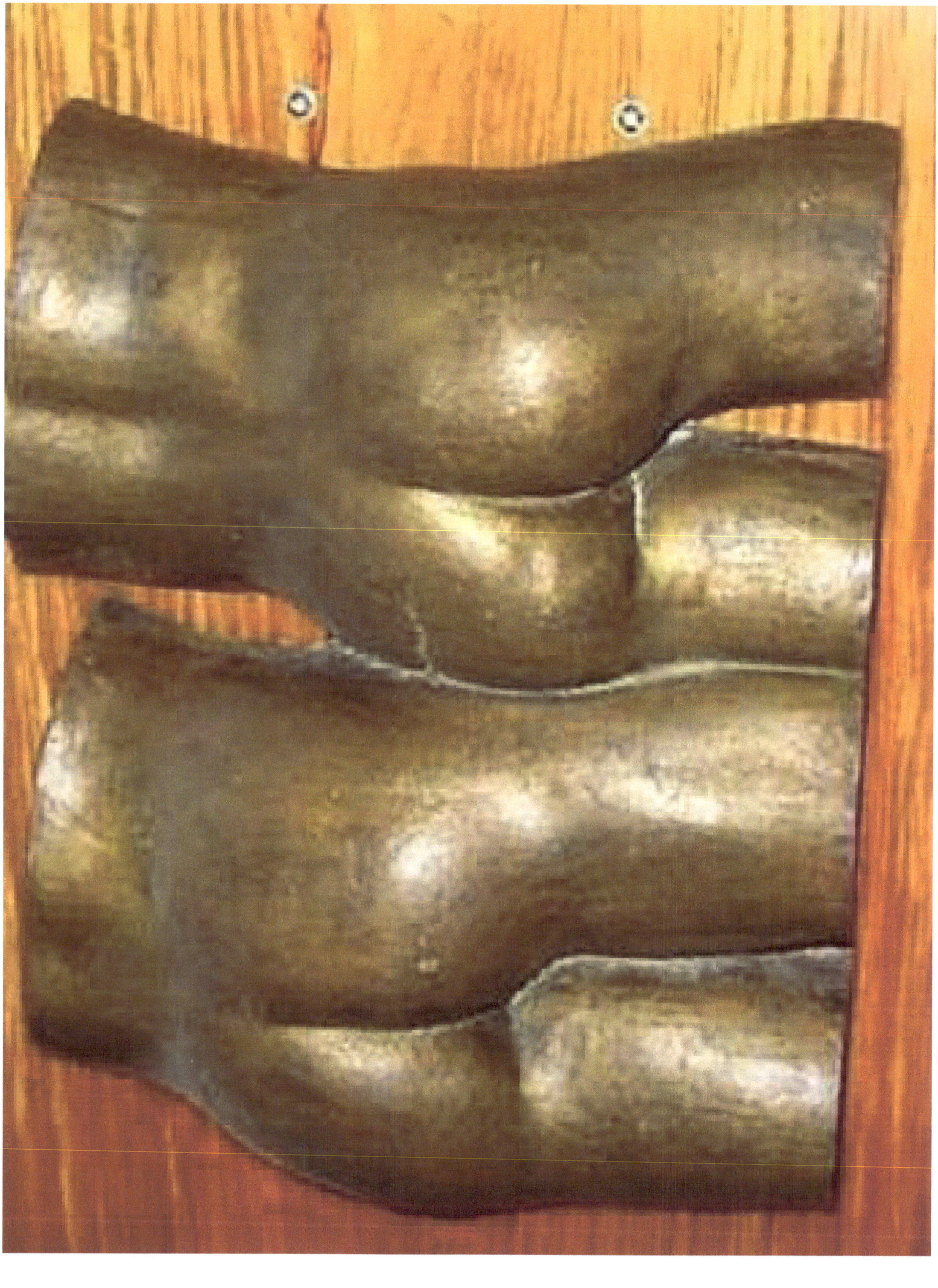

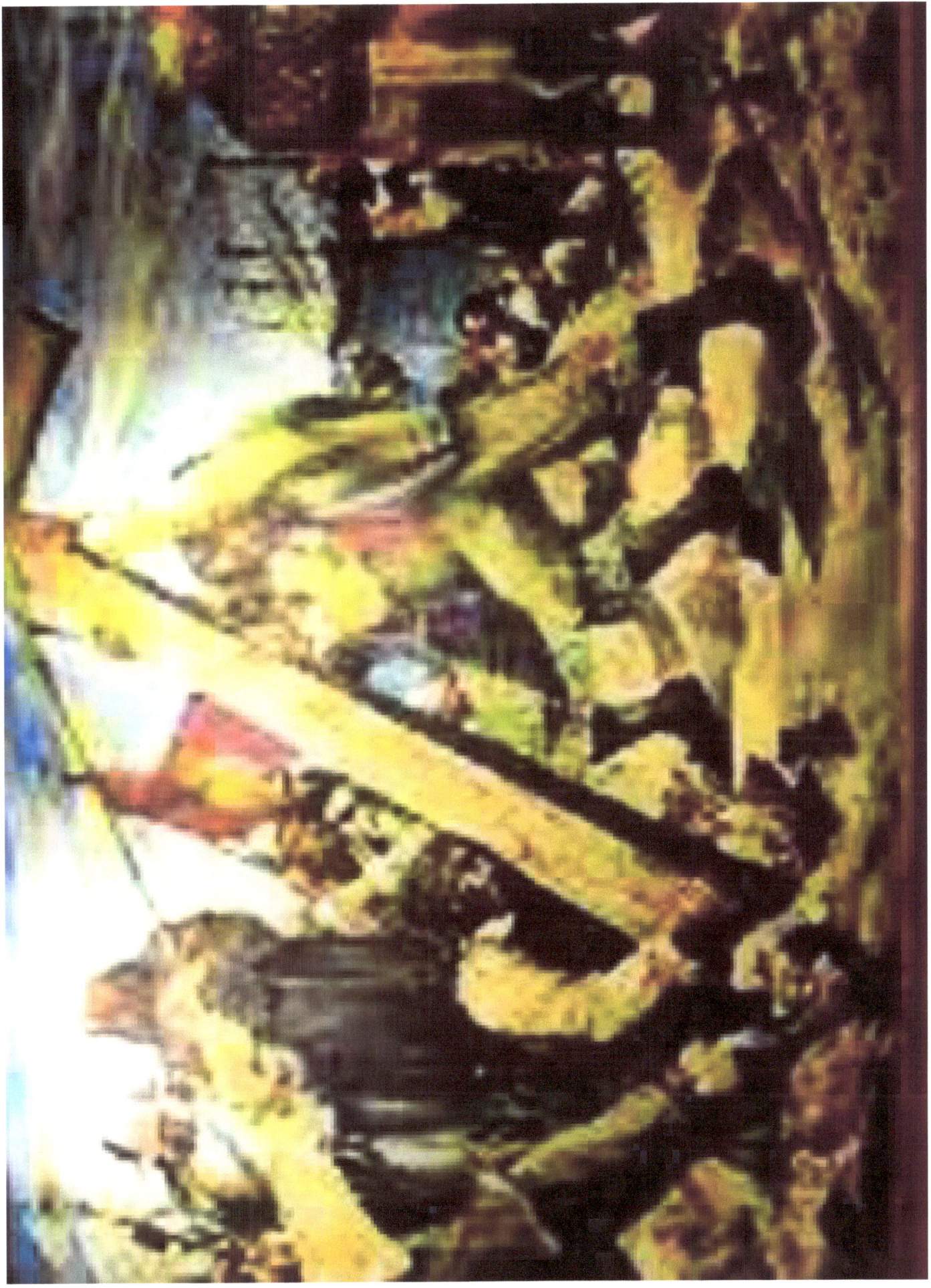

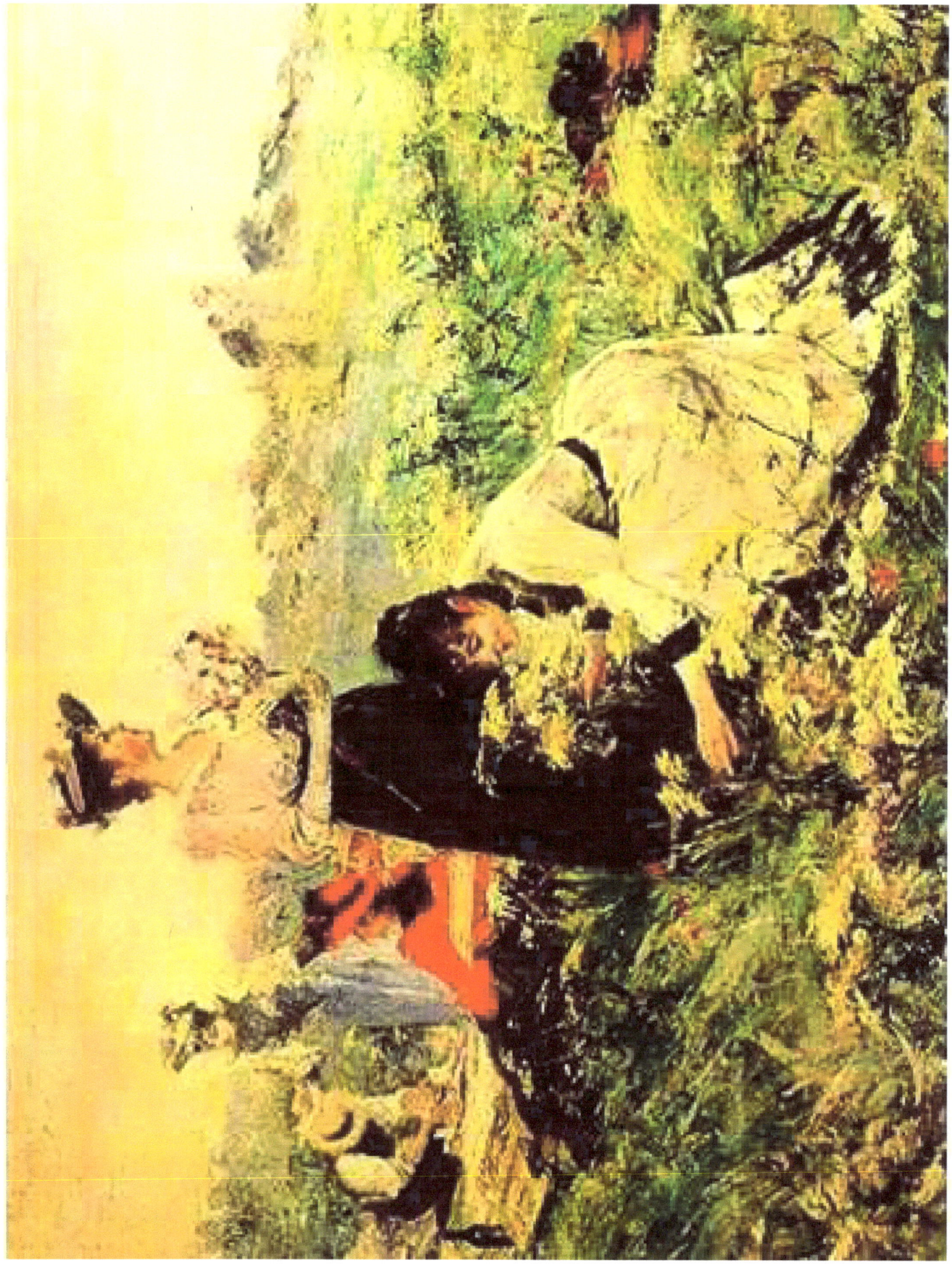

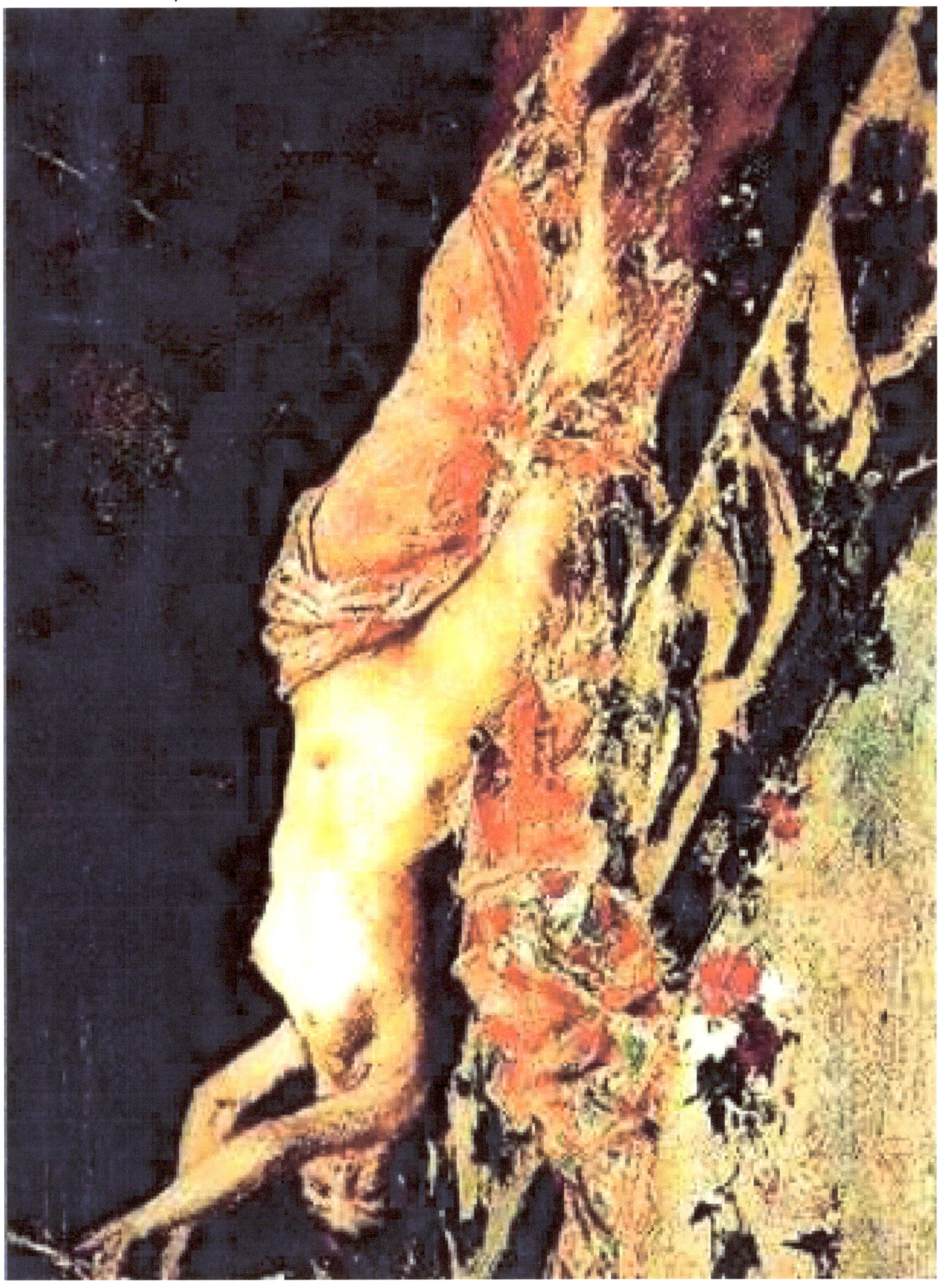

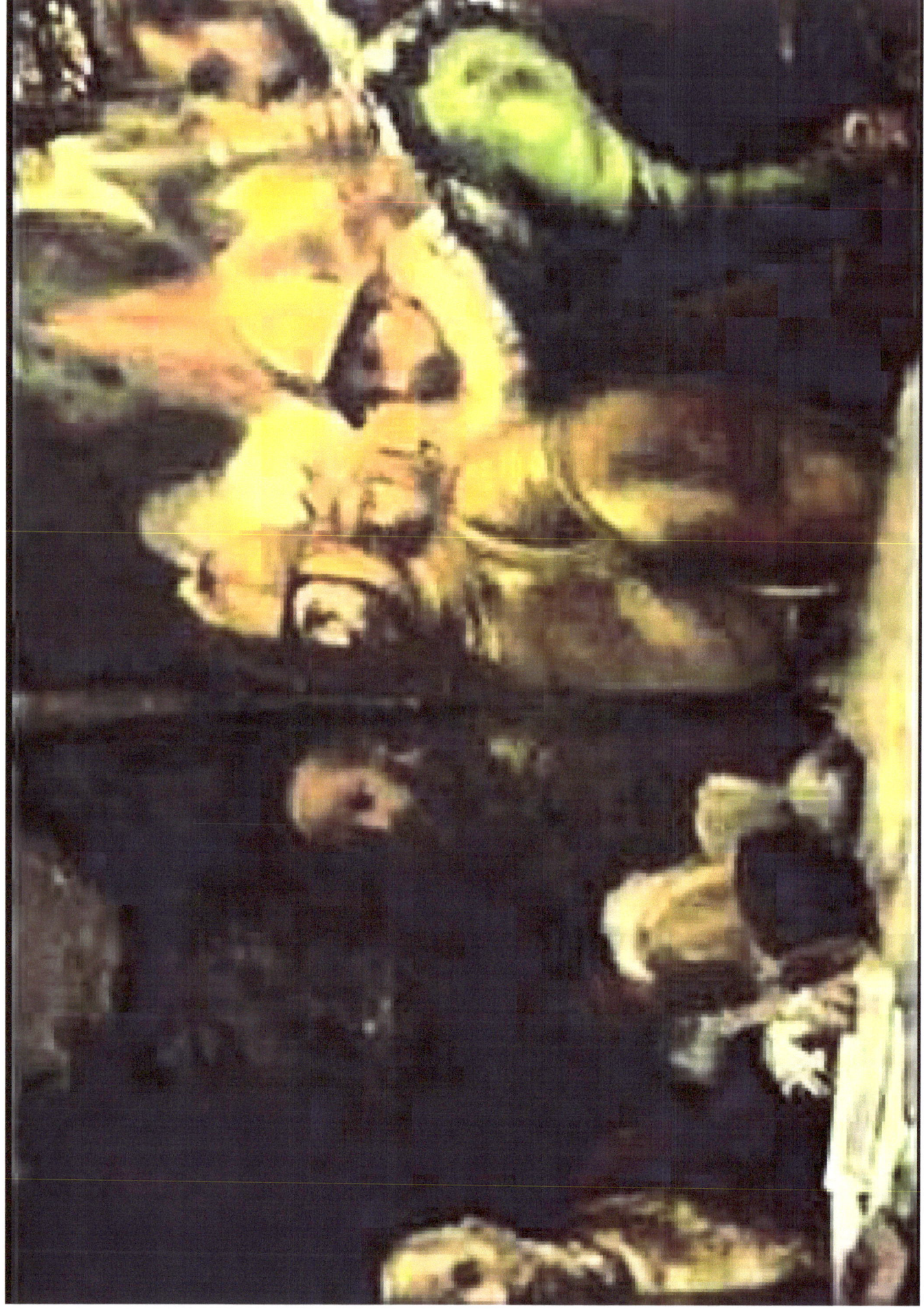

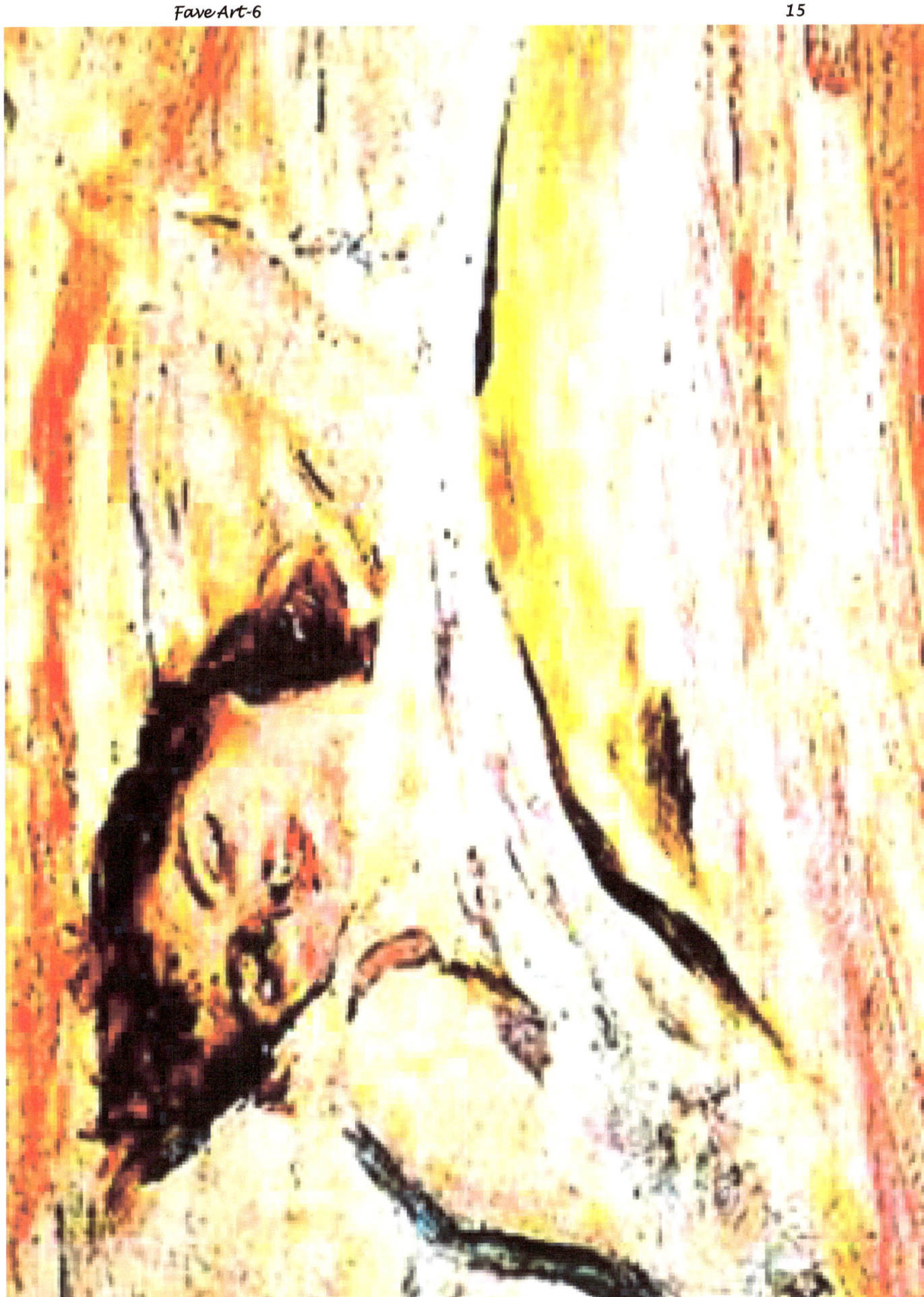

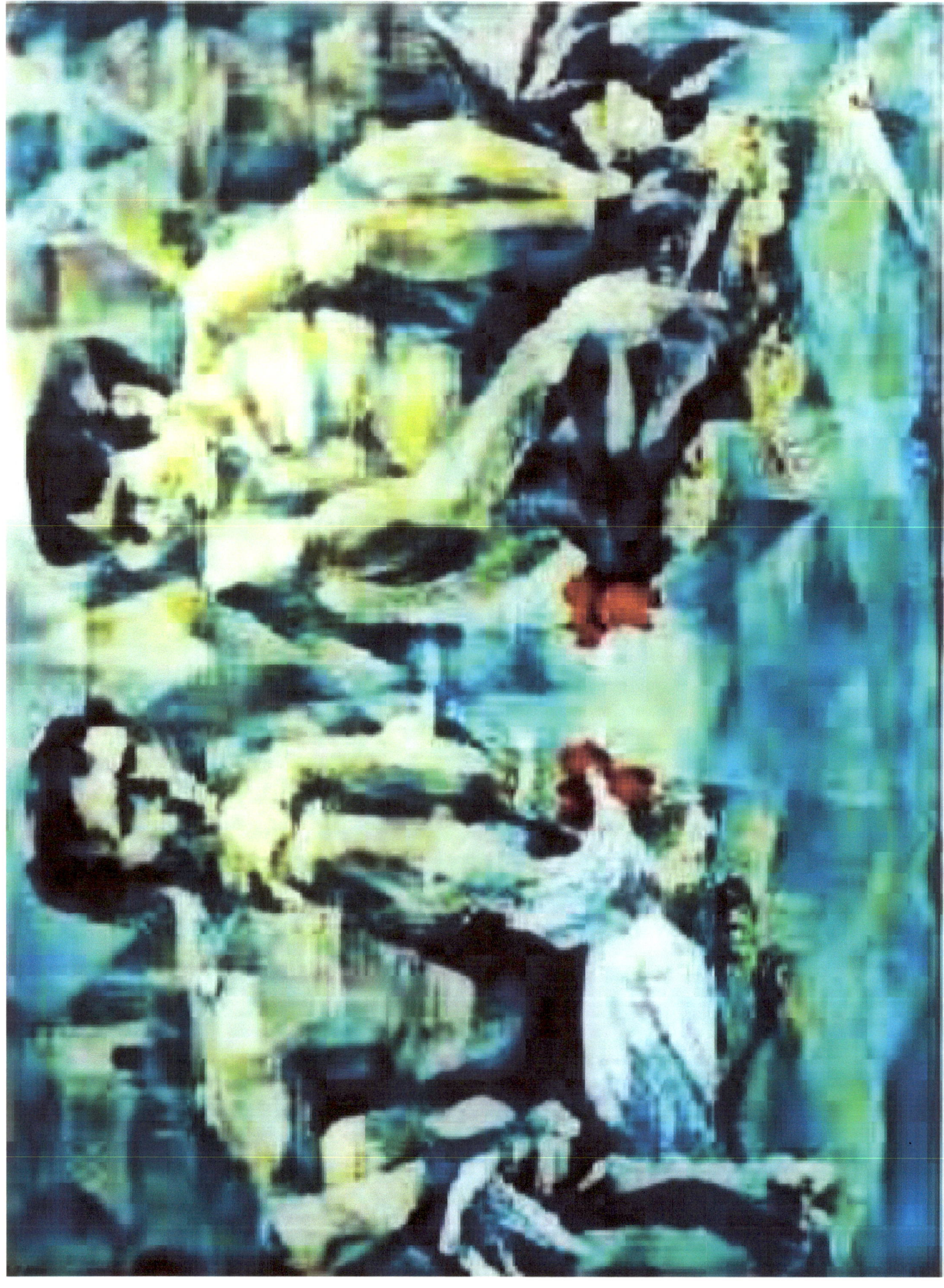

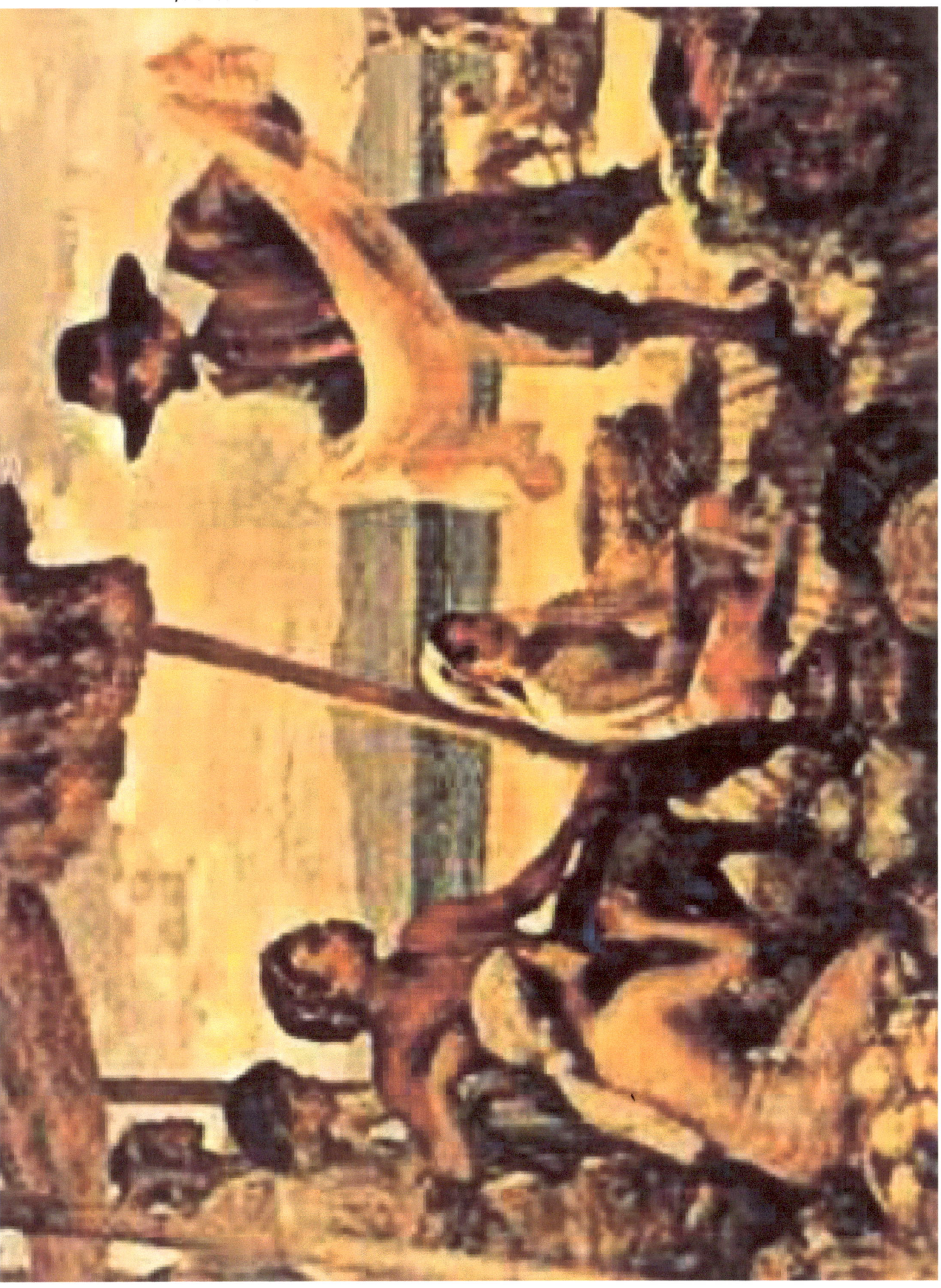

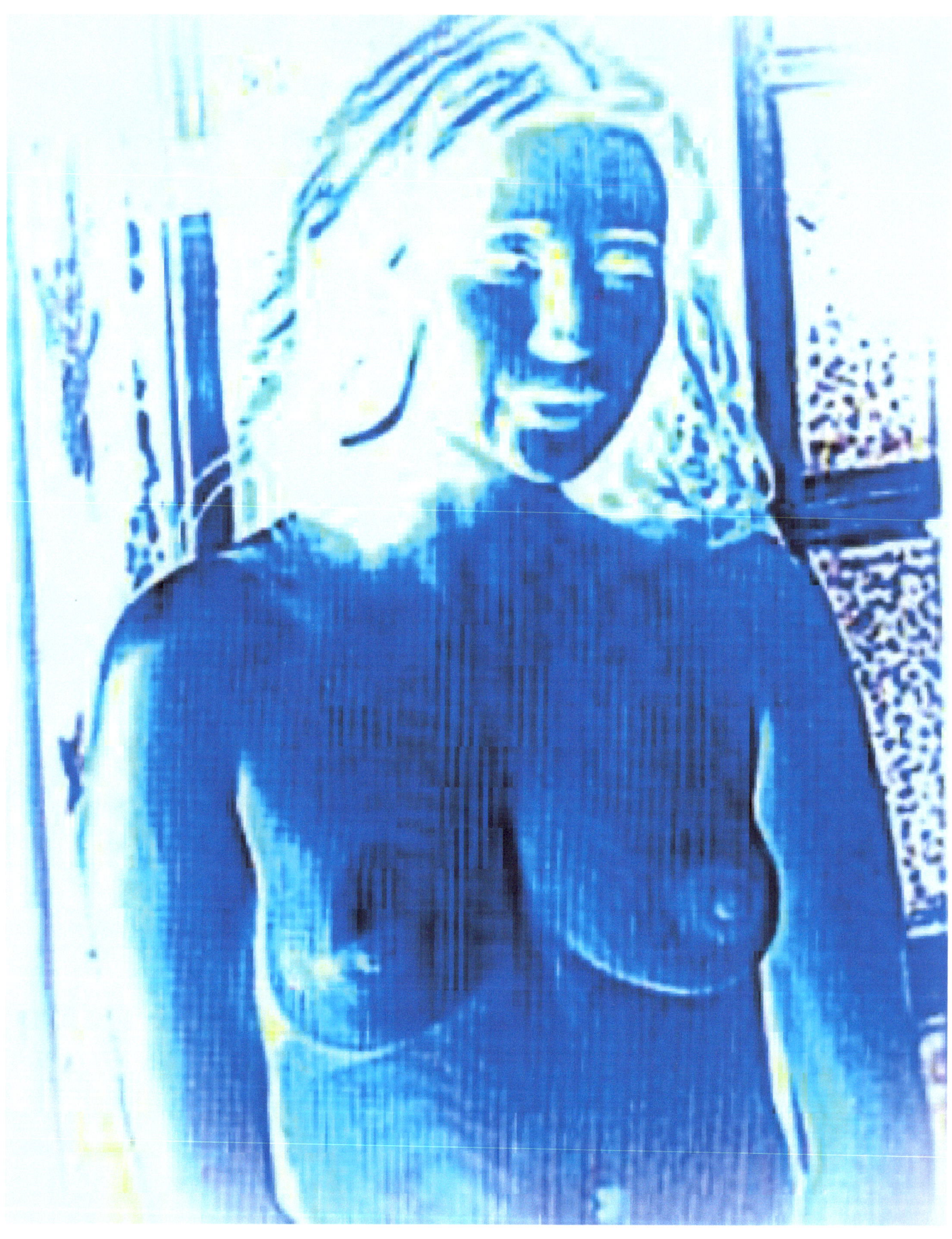

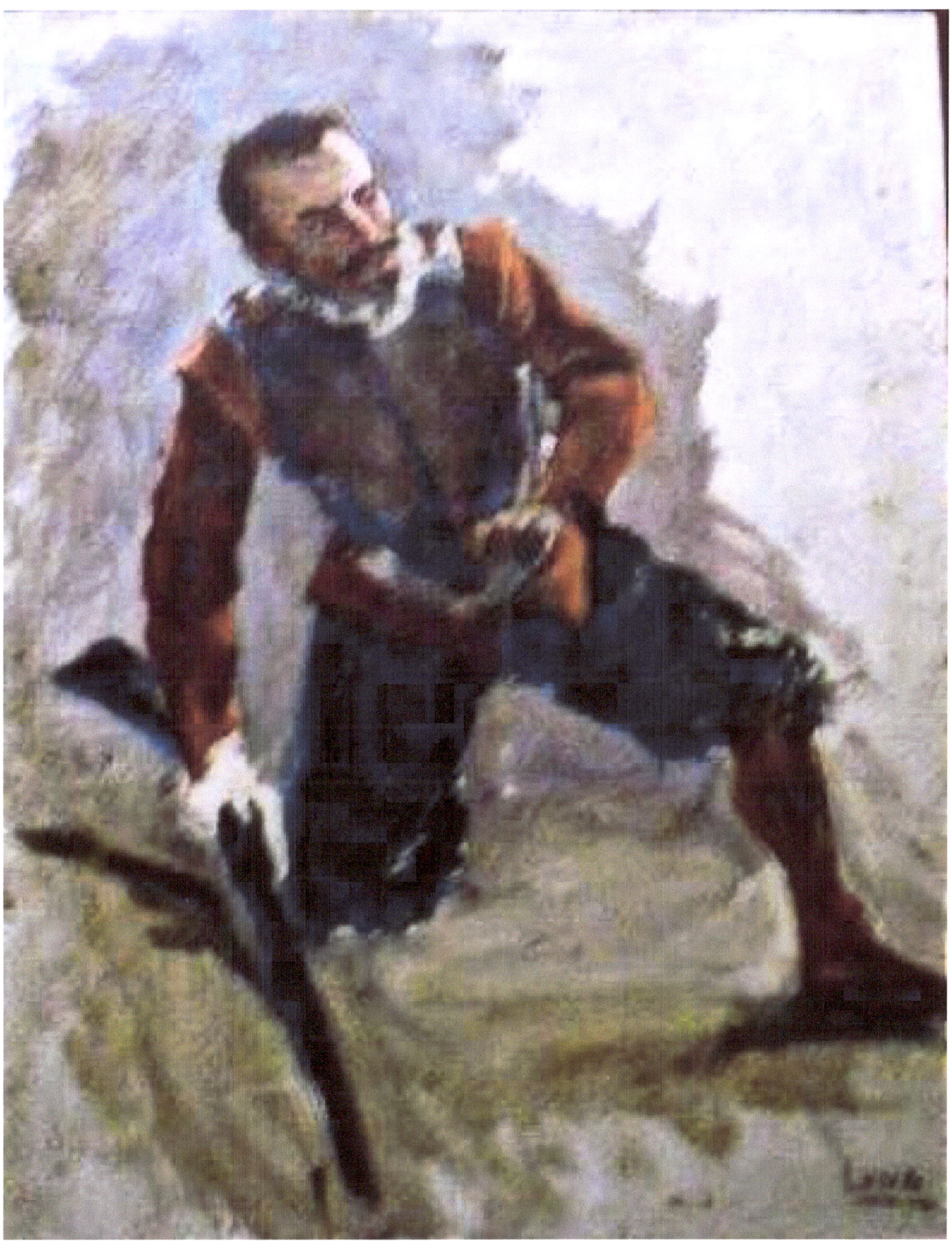

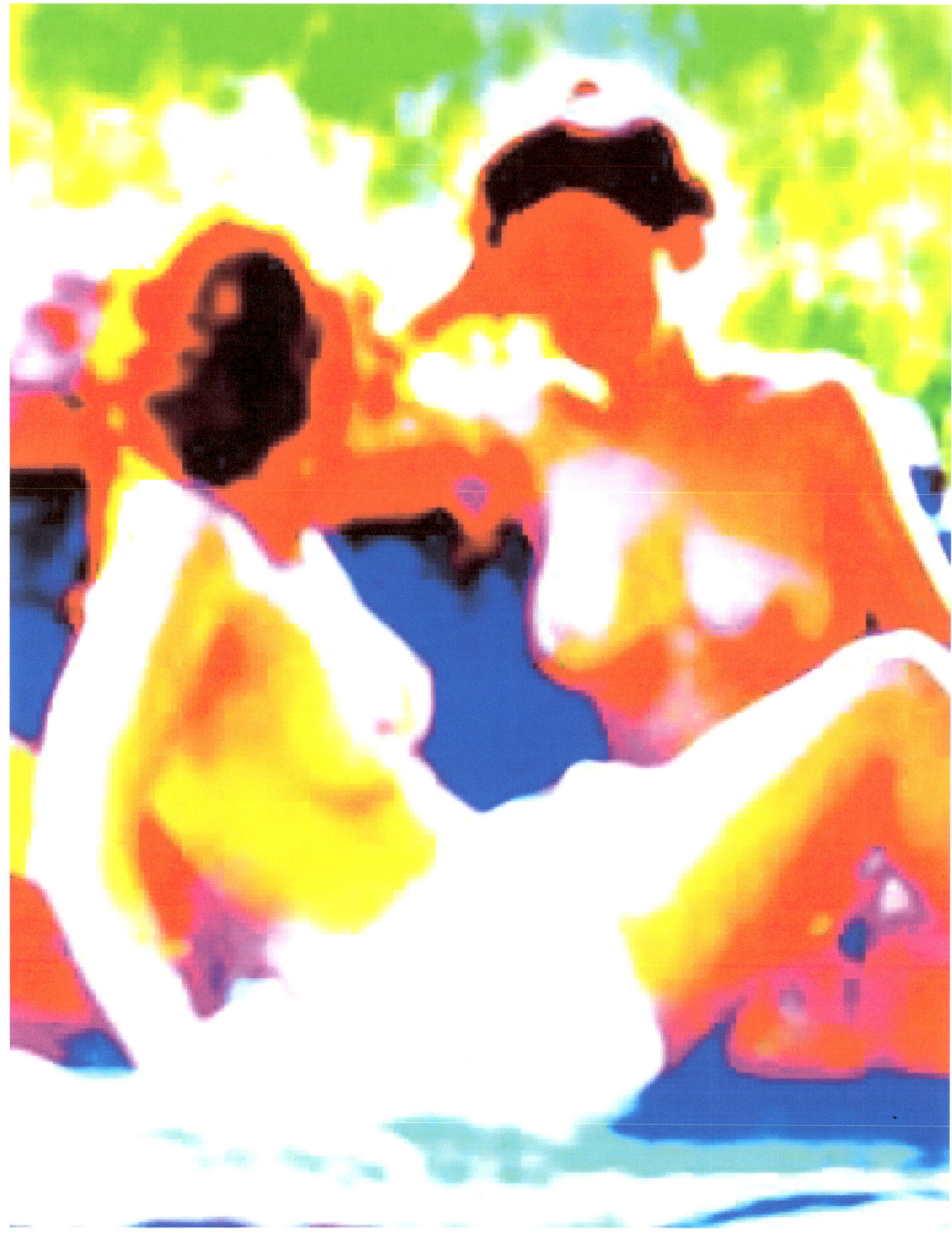

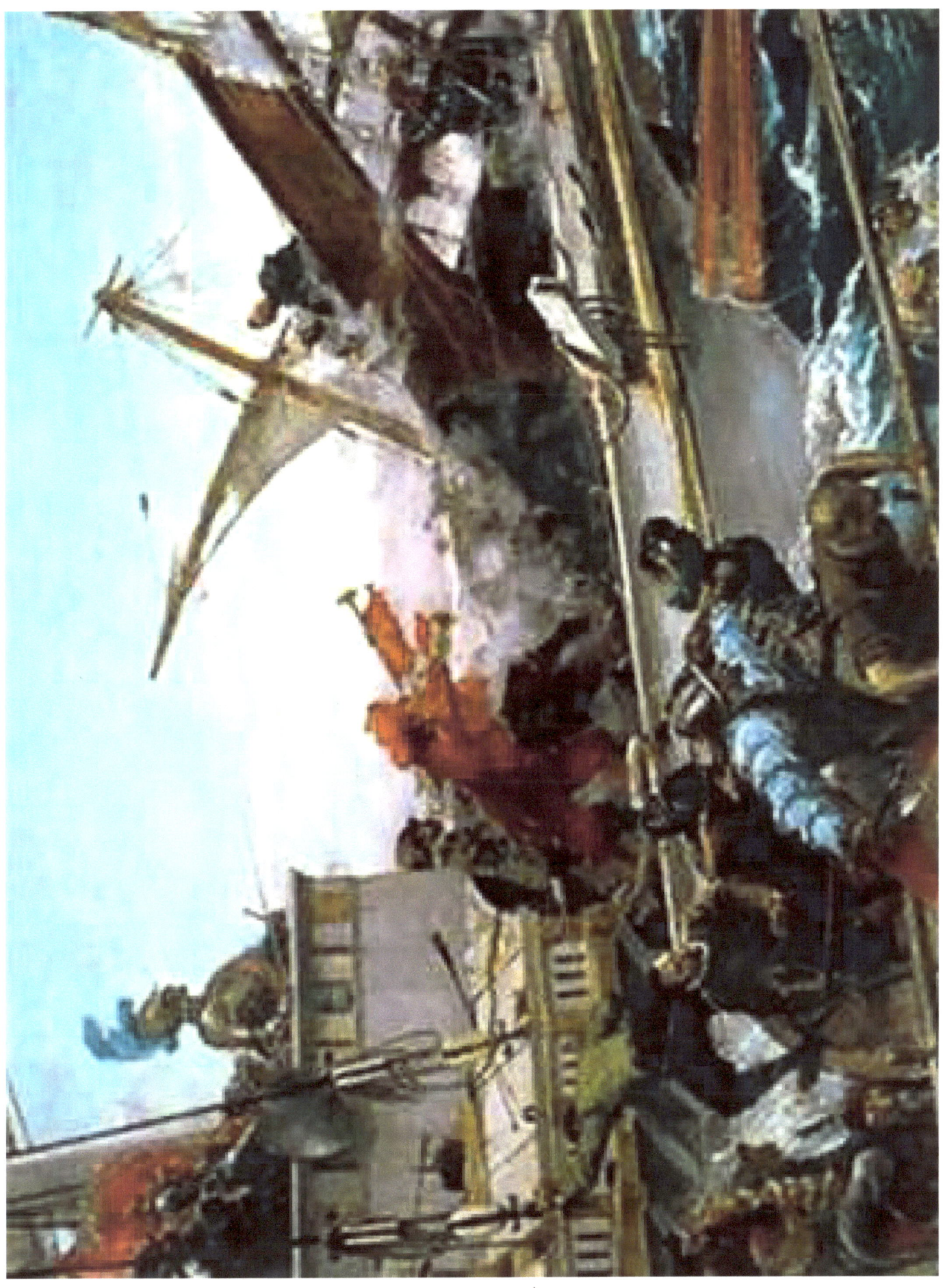

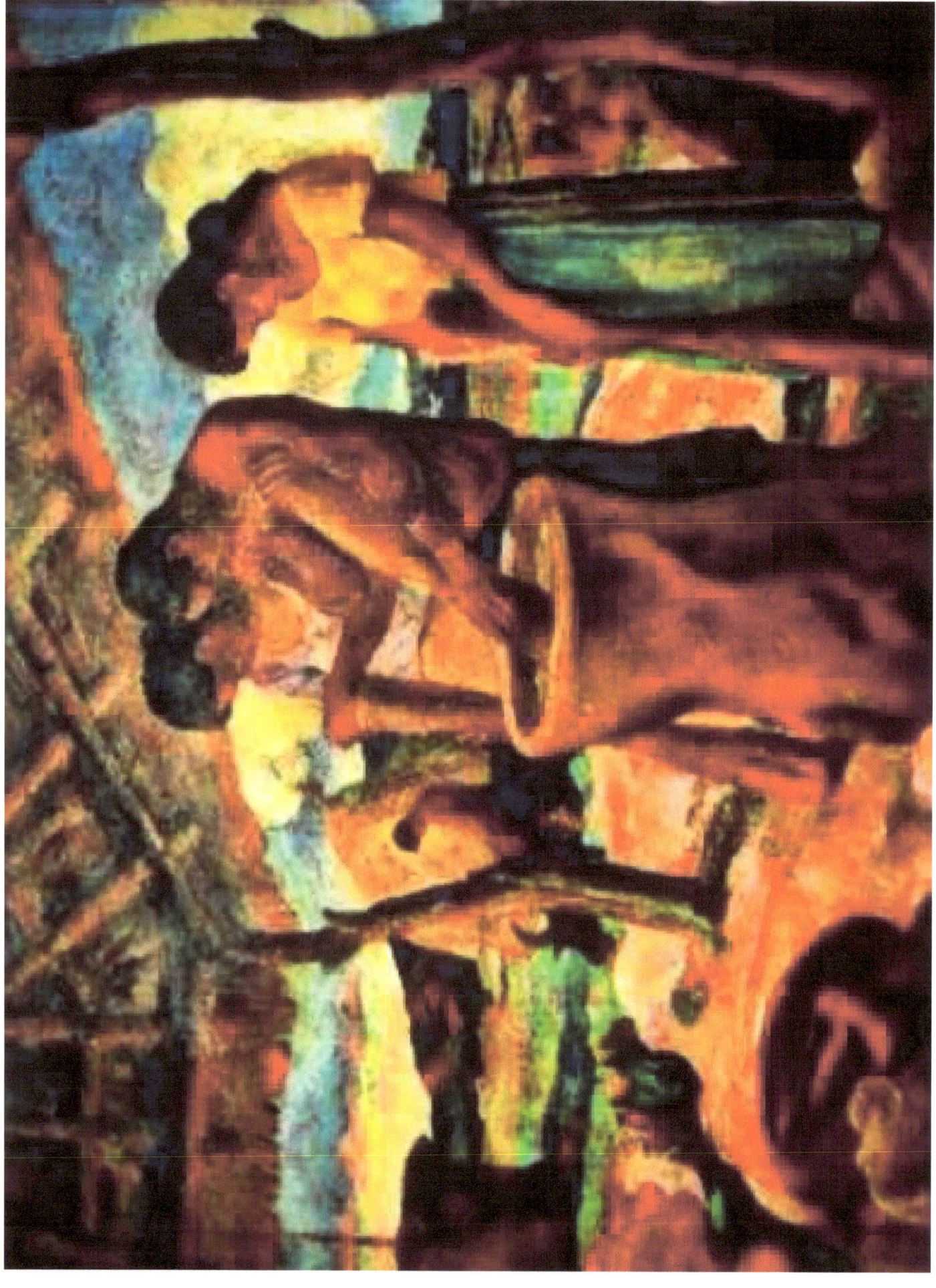

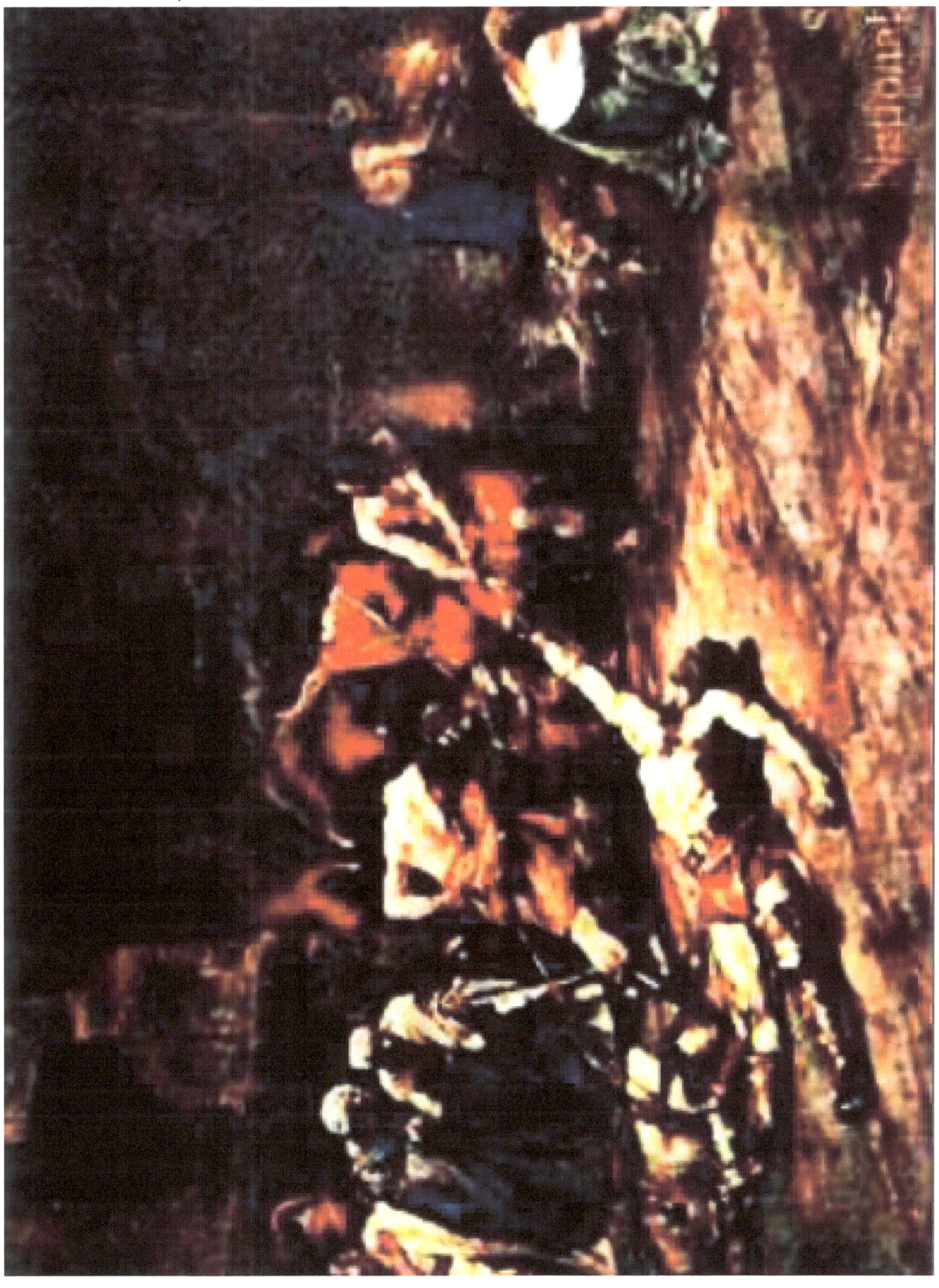

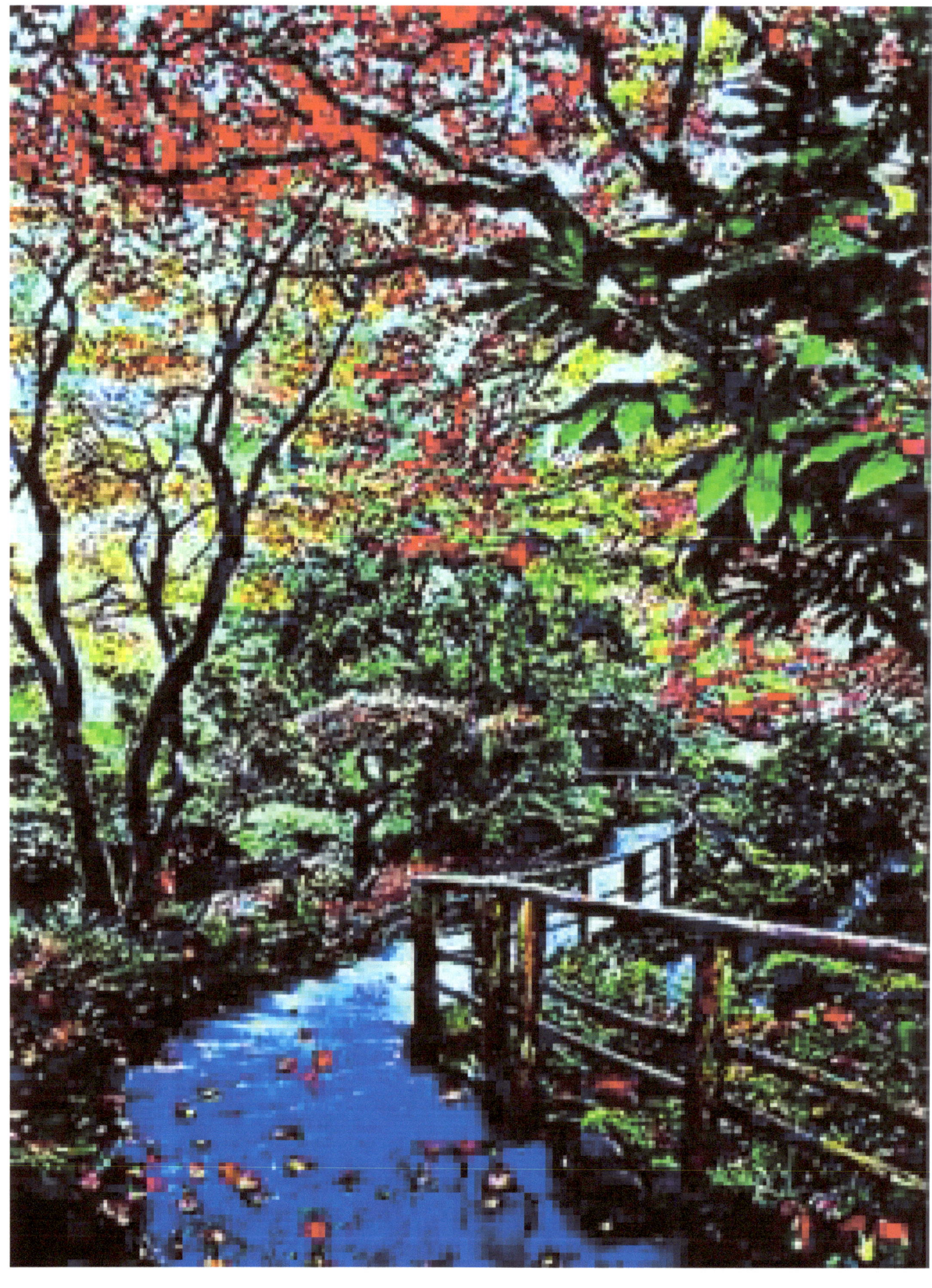

A Hermes Alegre Piece

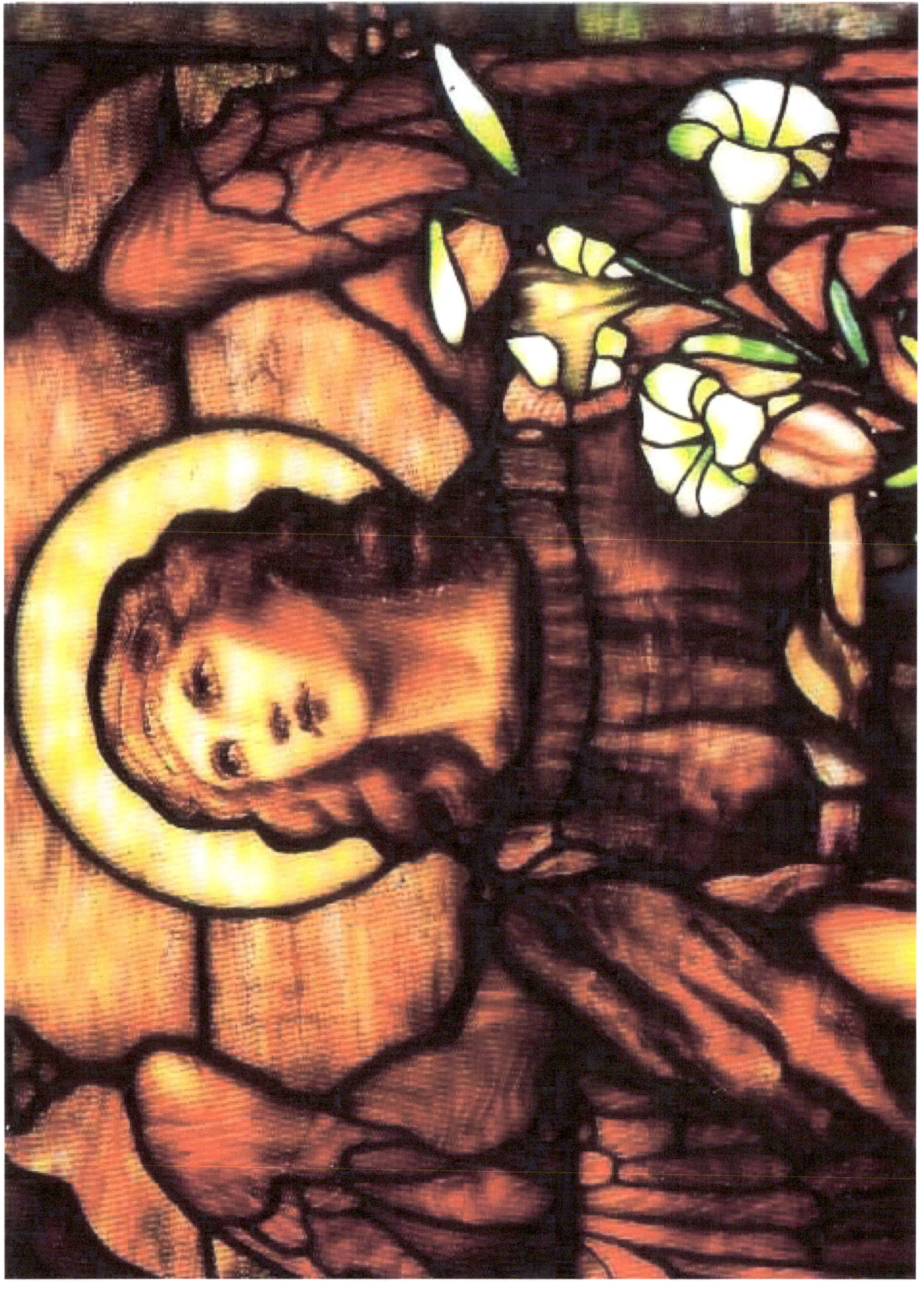

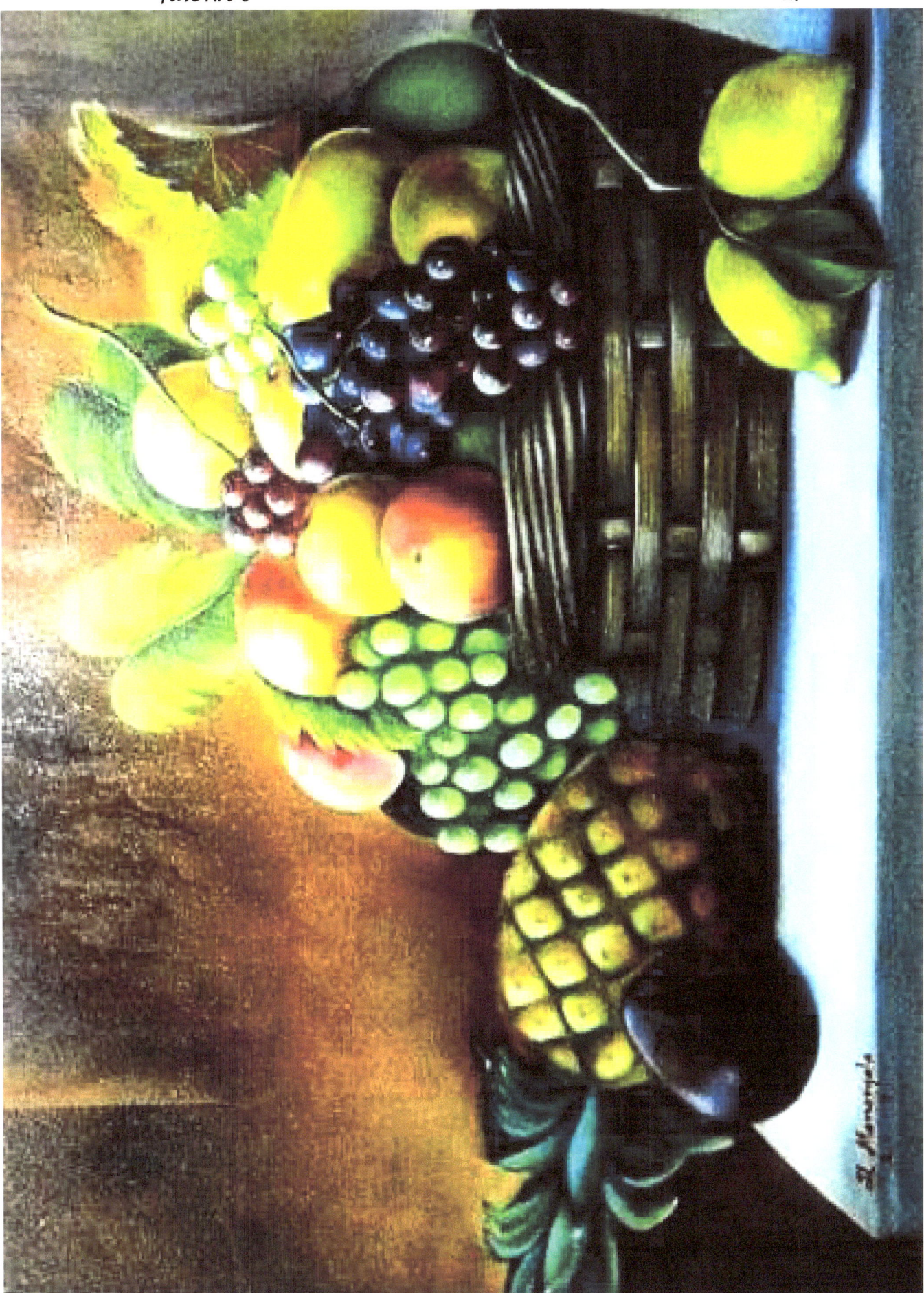

A Khristina Reed Manansala Piece

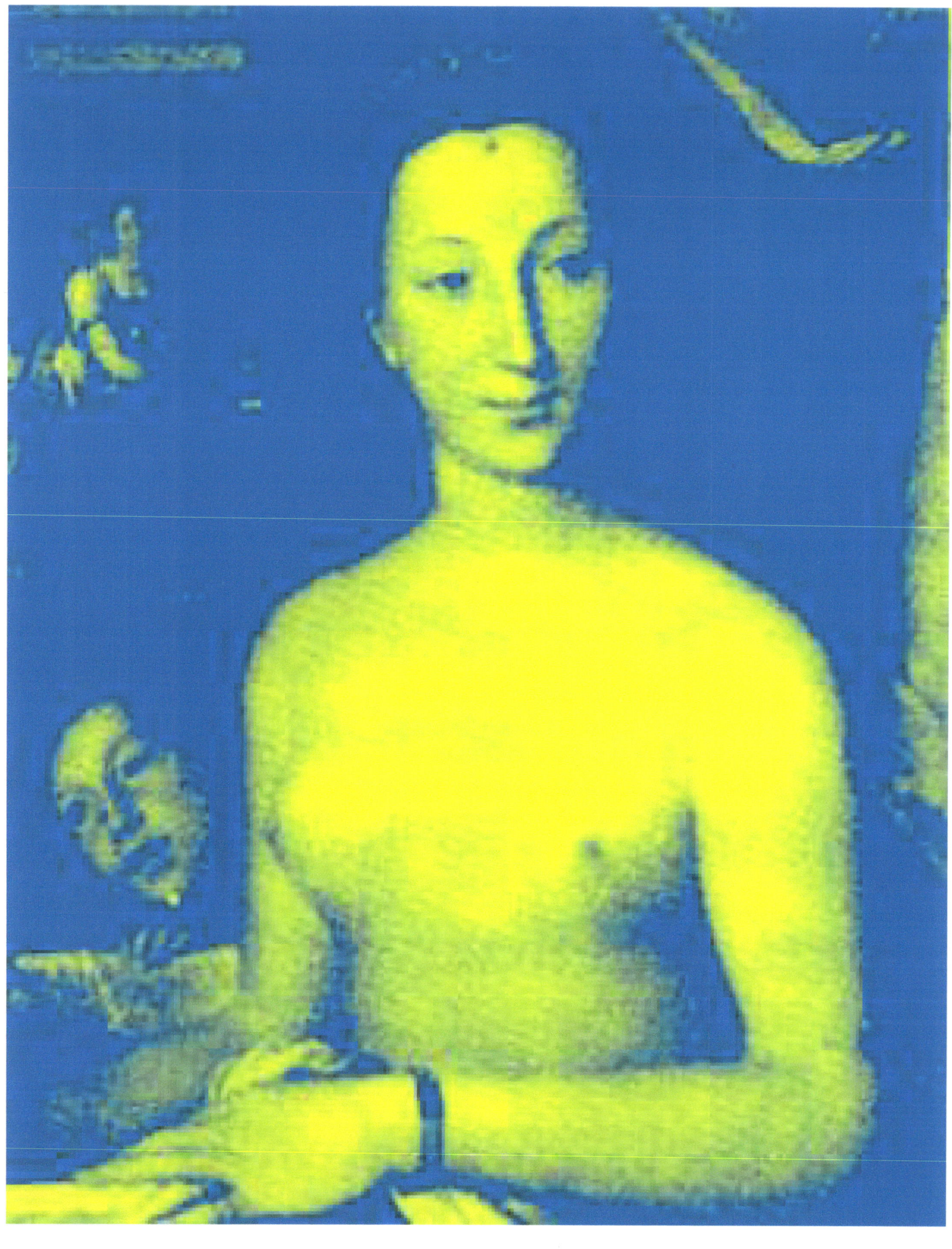

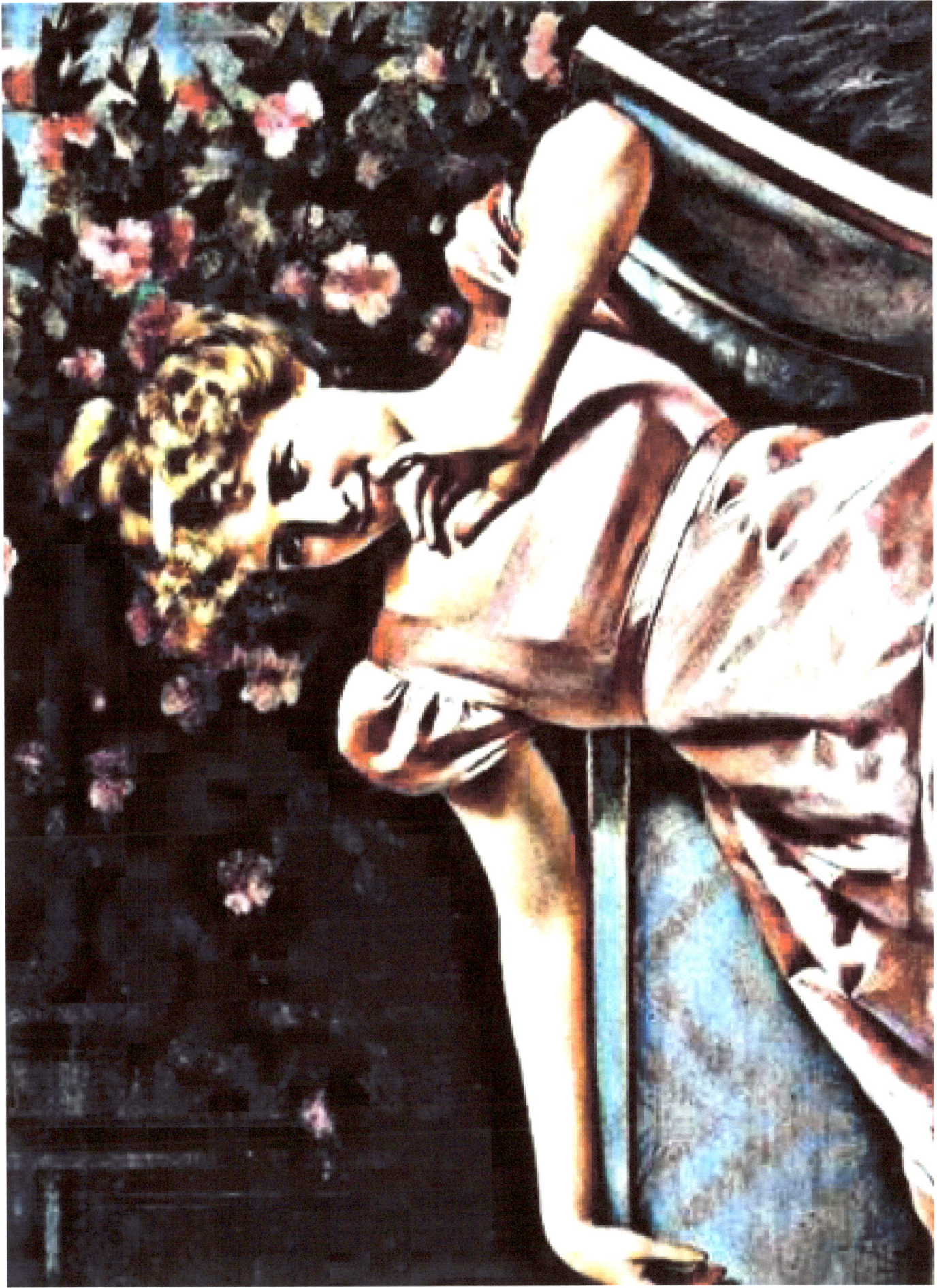

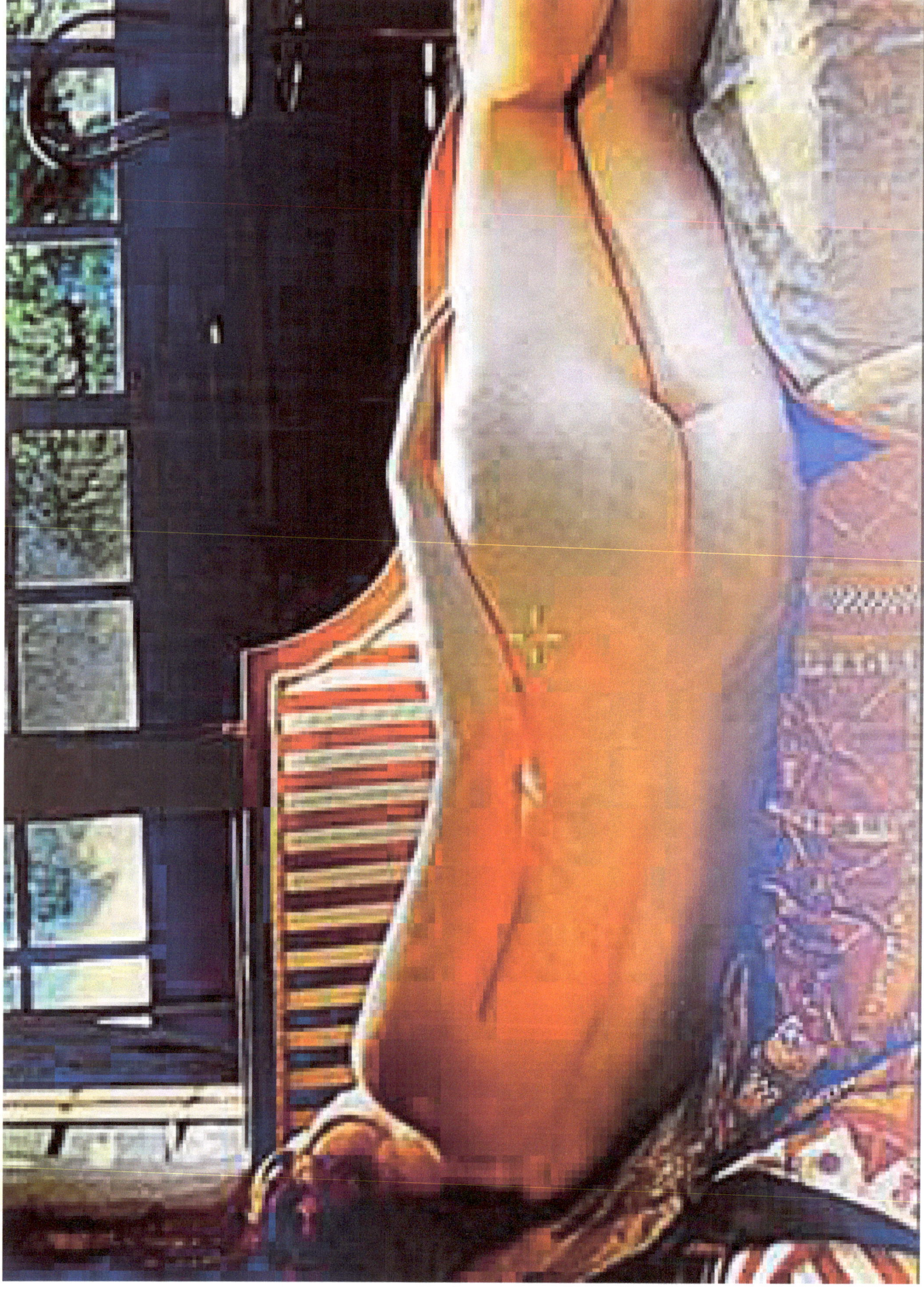

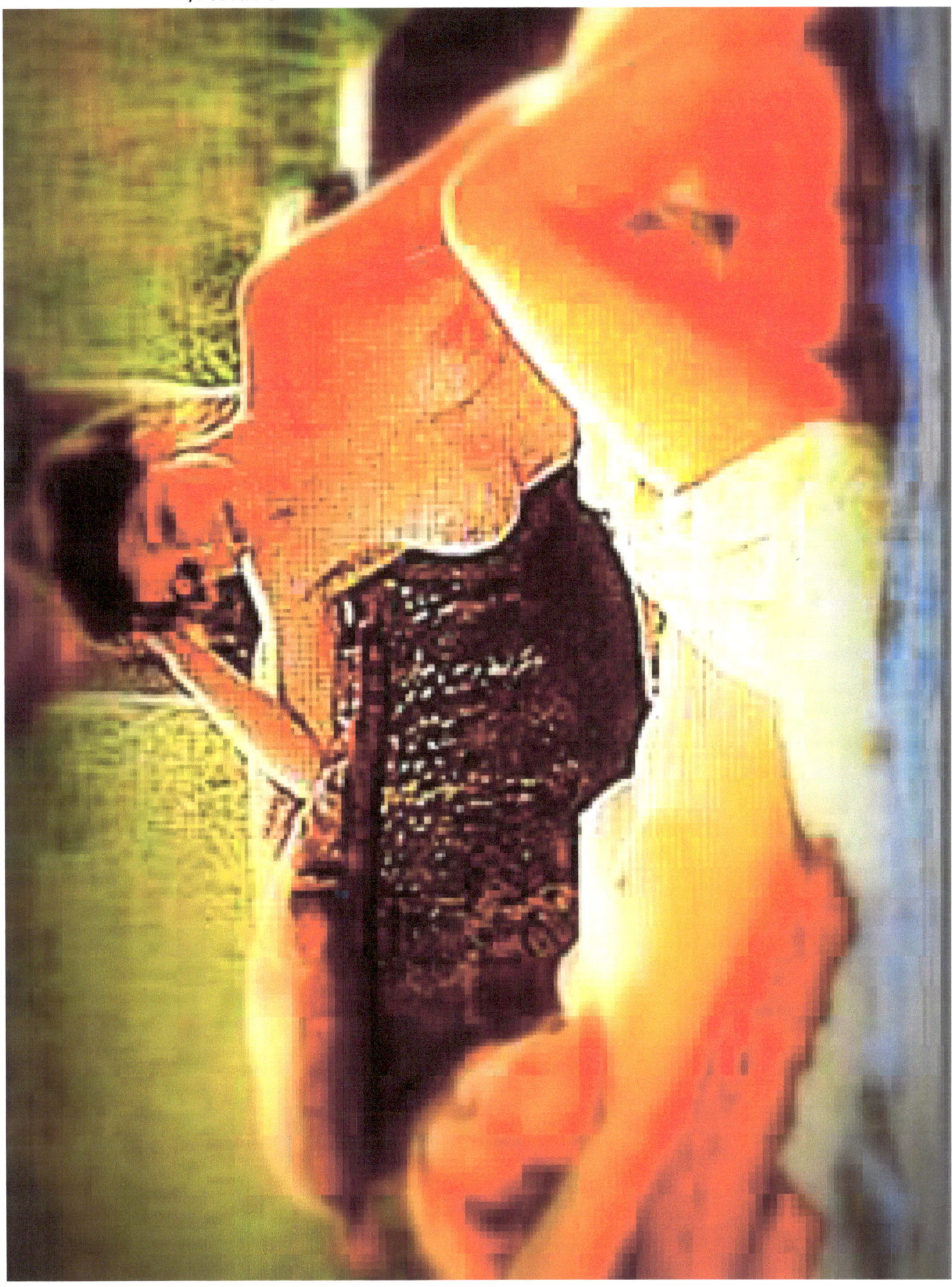

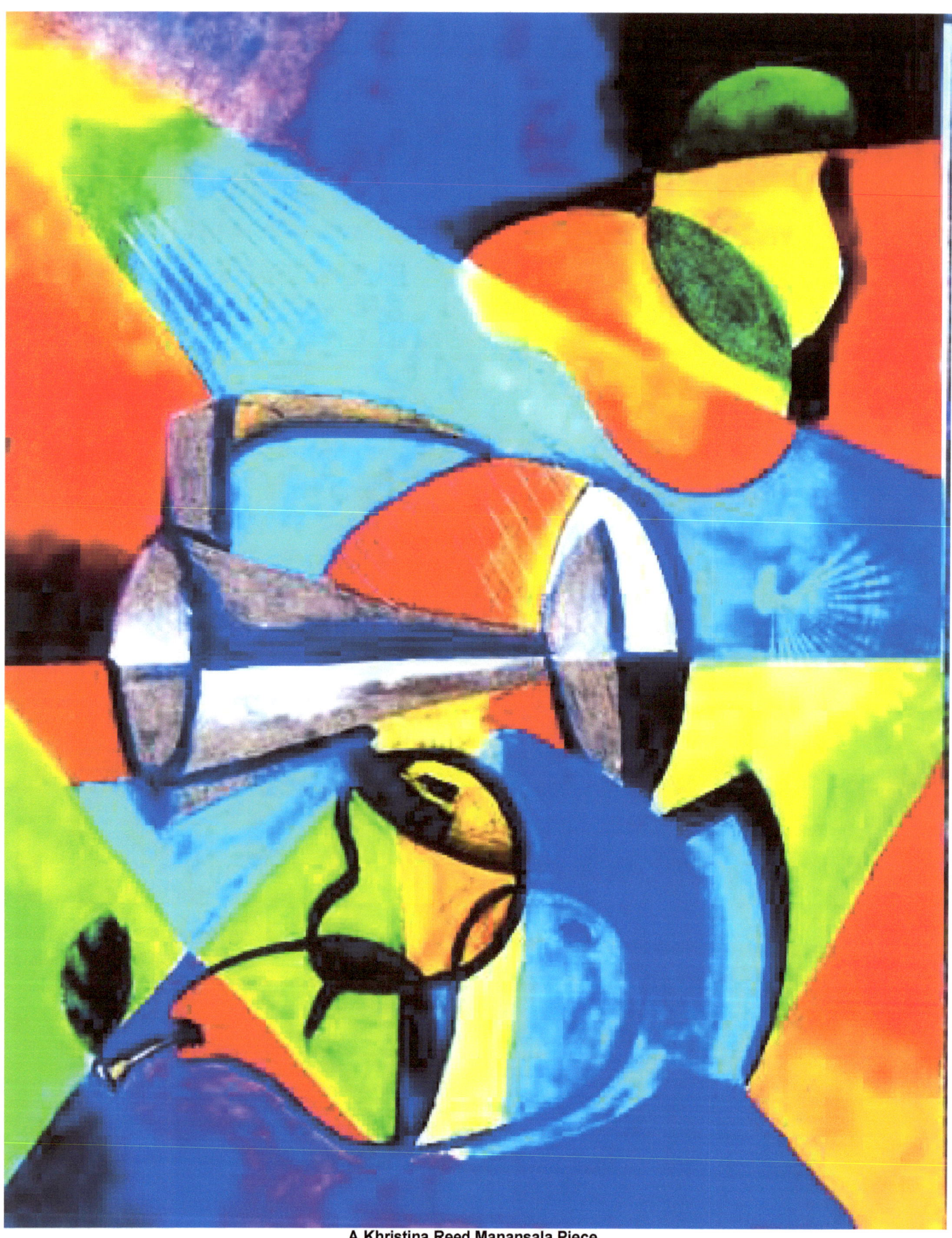

A Khristina Reed Manansala Piece

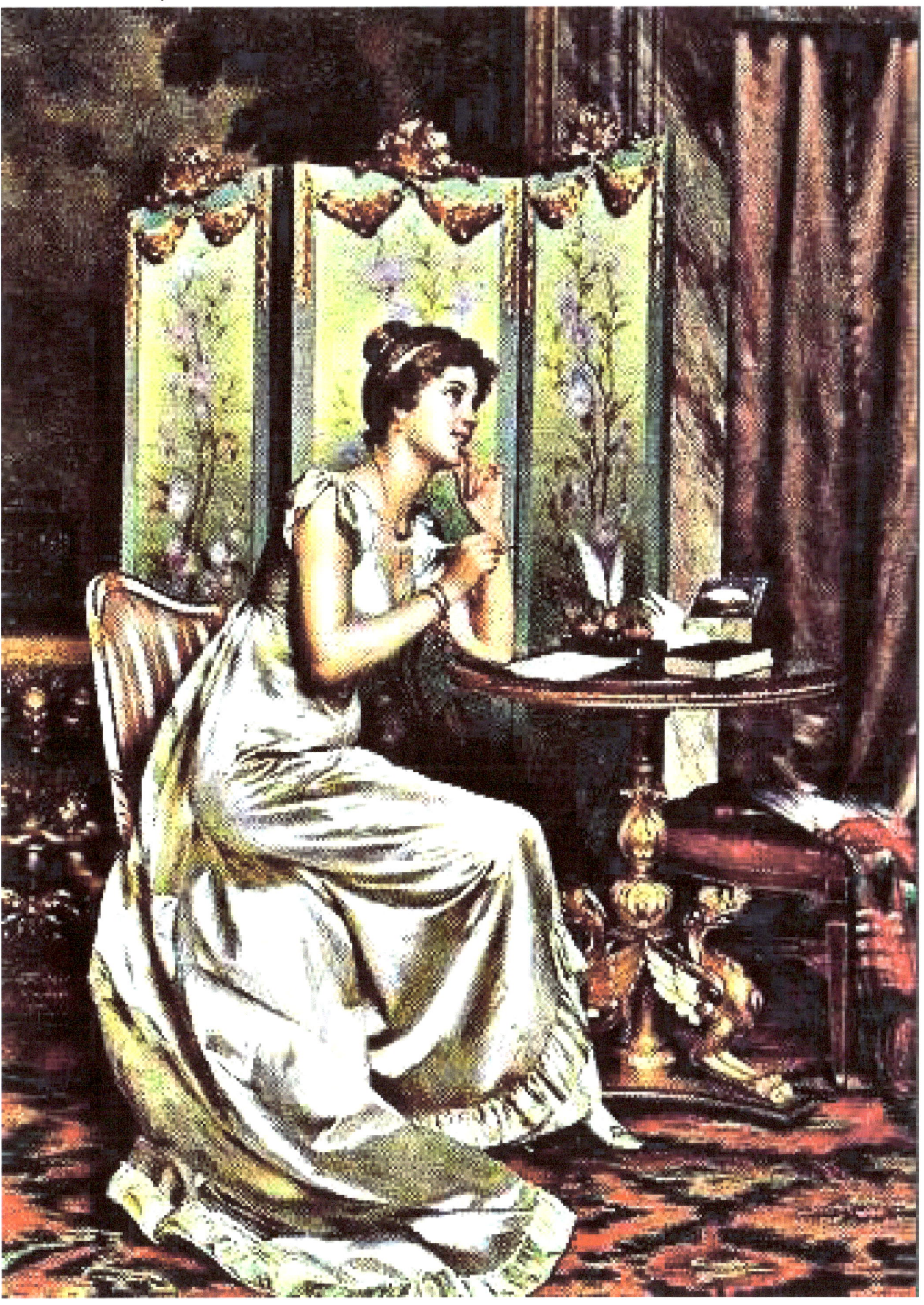

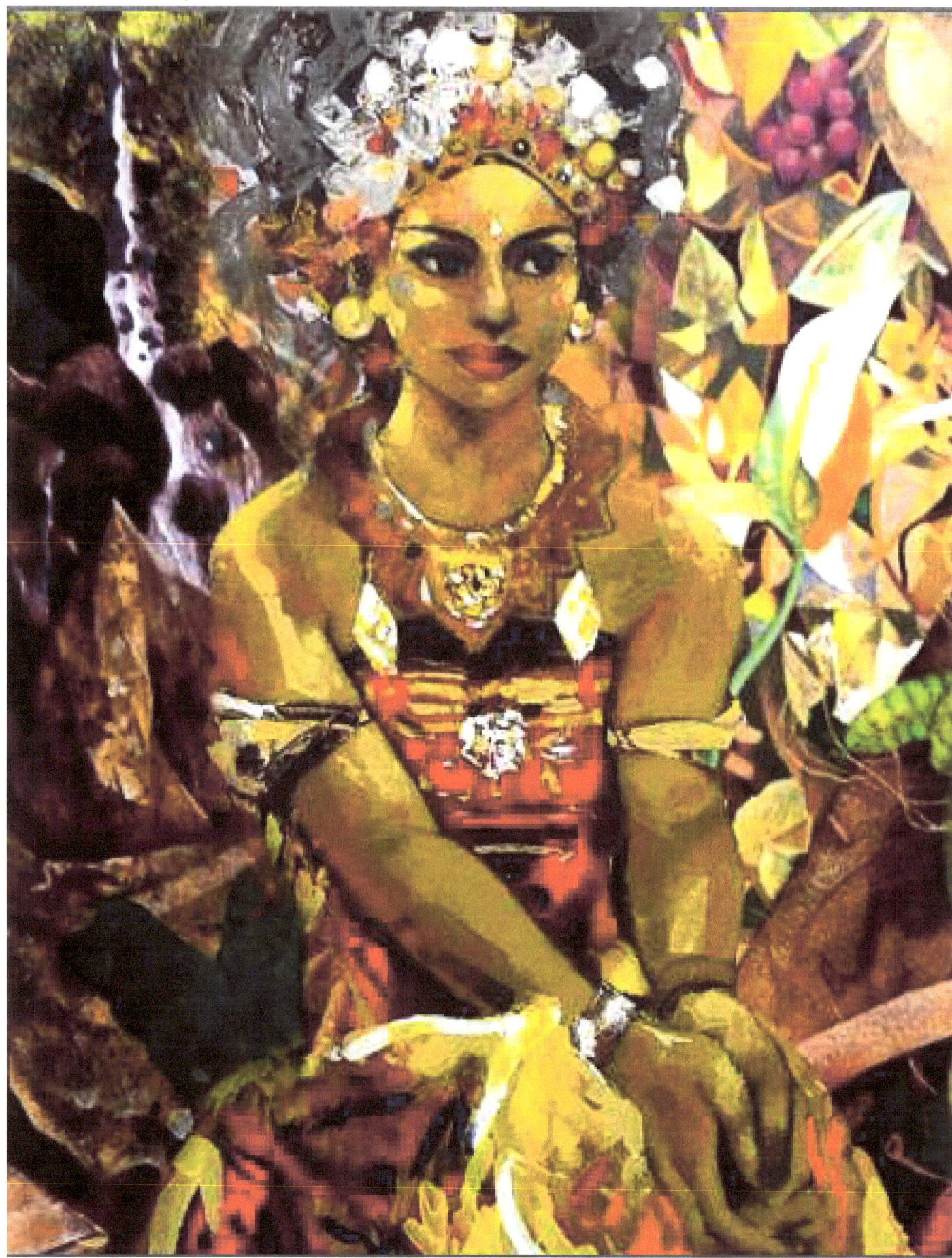

A Hermes Alegre Piece

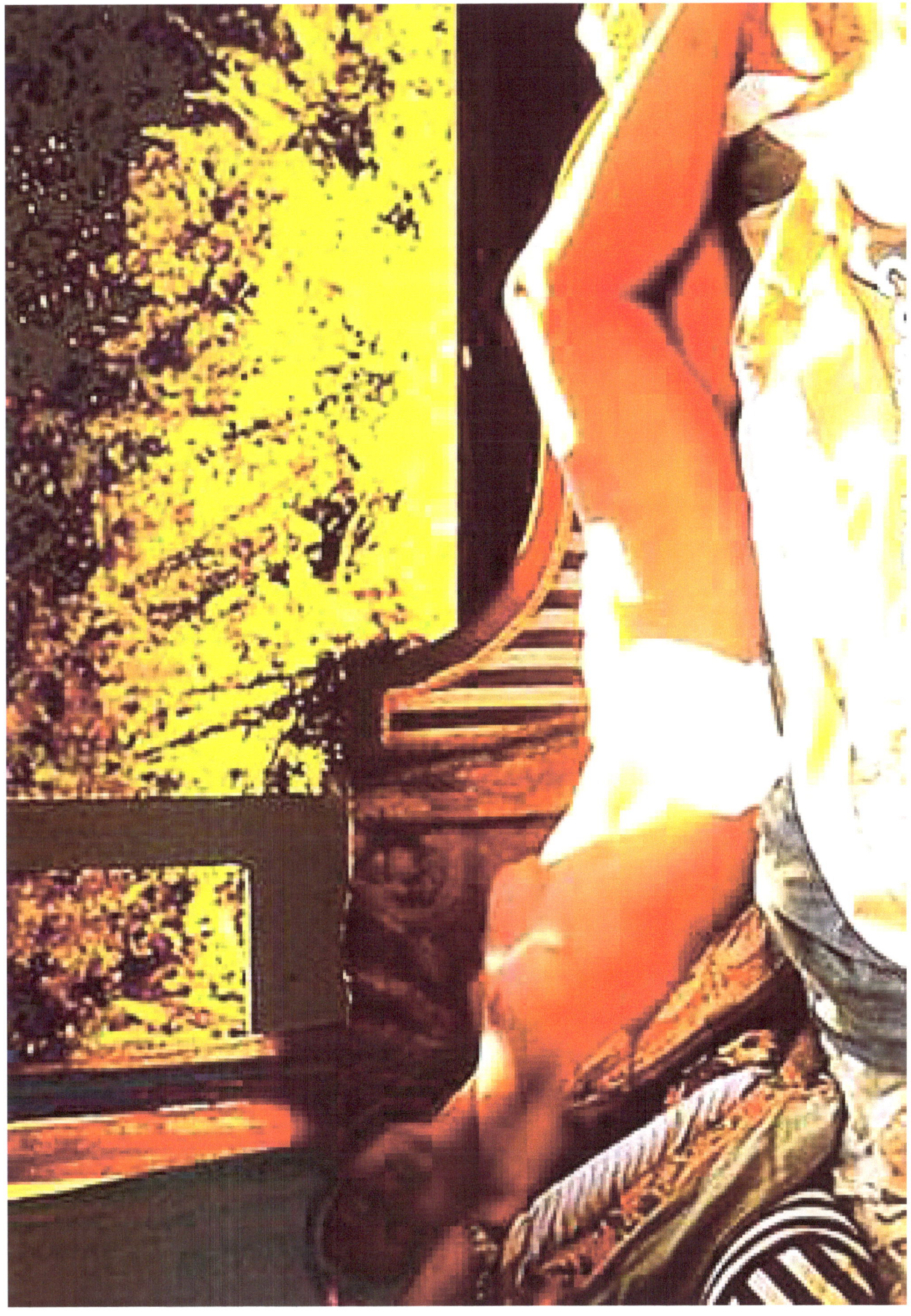

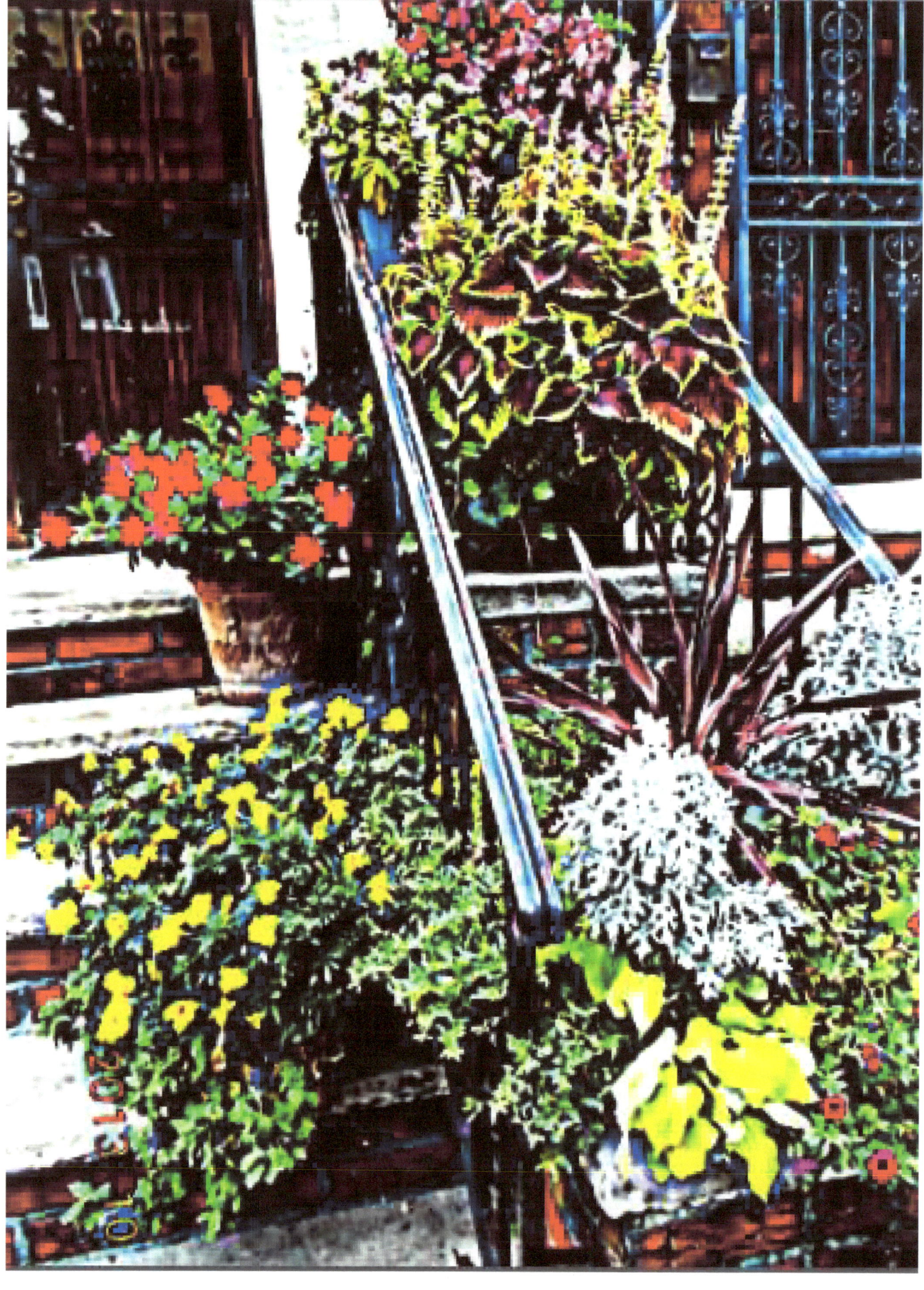

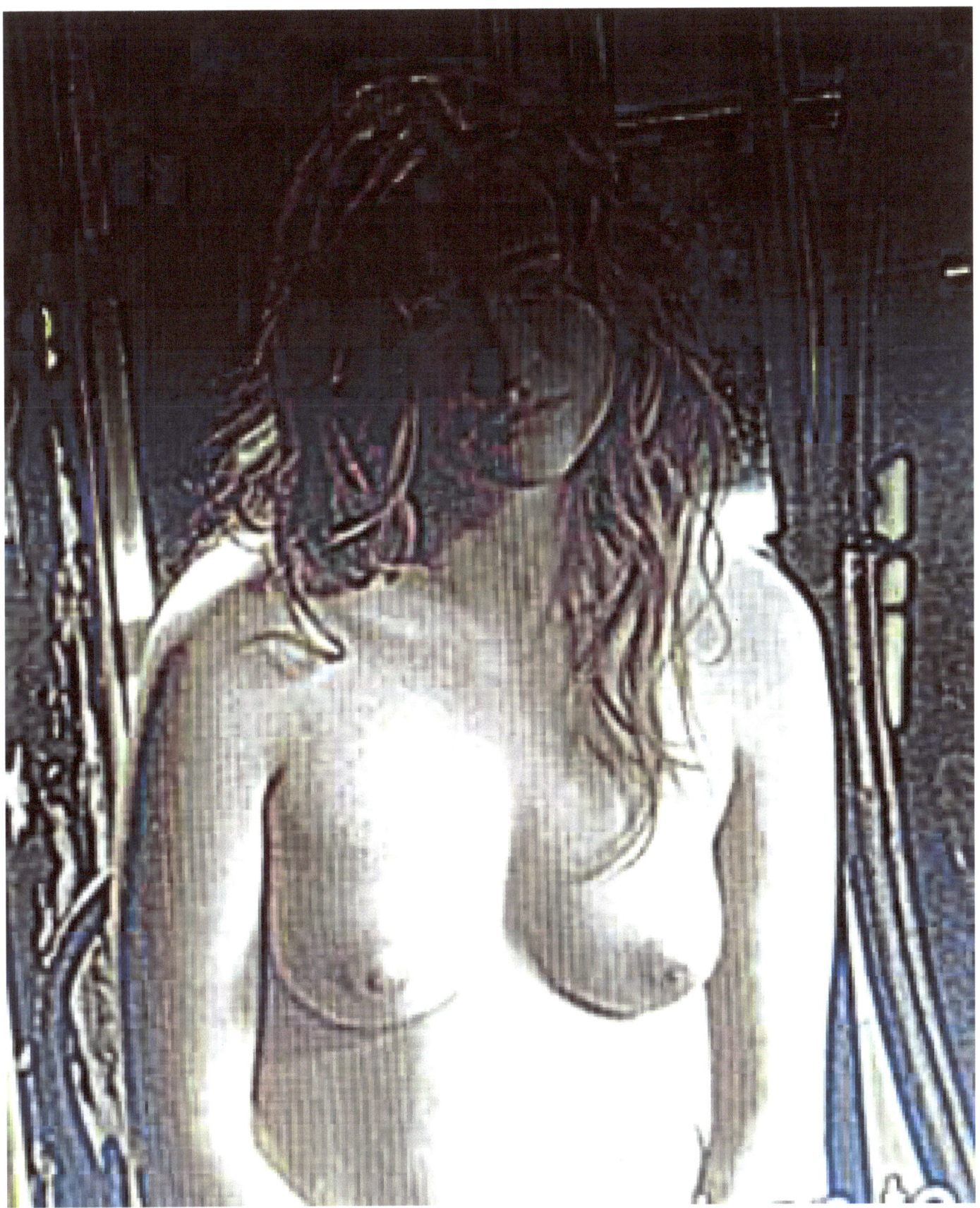

WELCOME! We hope you enjoy this Fave Art-6 collection of my favorite art works. Most art works are copied from the internet, posters, pictures and books. They are computer-generated and enhanced digitally. You may display this book as coffee table book in your living room, as conversation piece. You may give this book as gift. You may cut out and frame each page. Each art work is 8.5x11 inches and suitable for framing, and then wall decors.

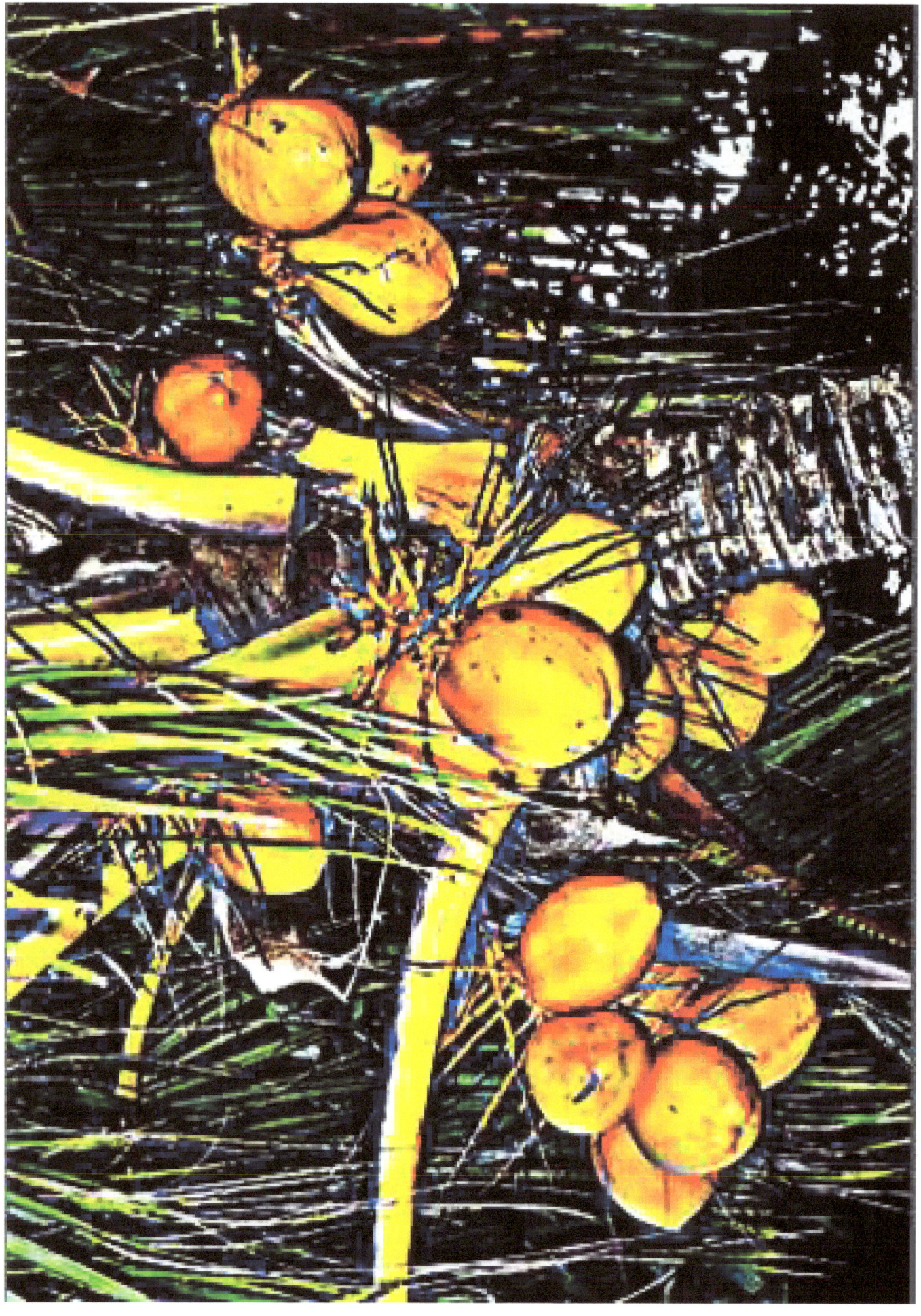

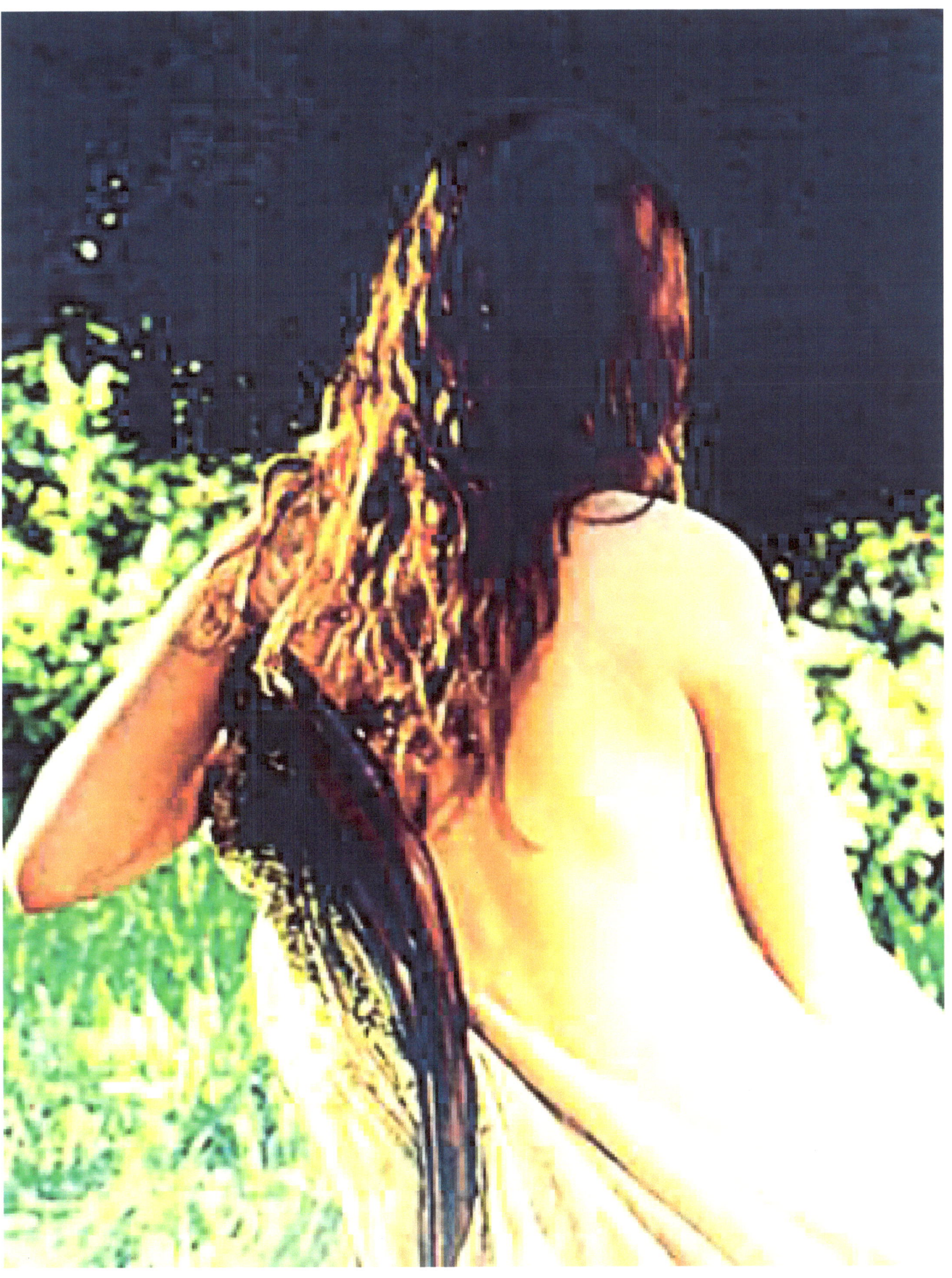

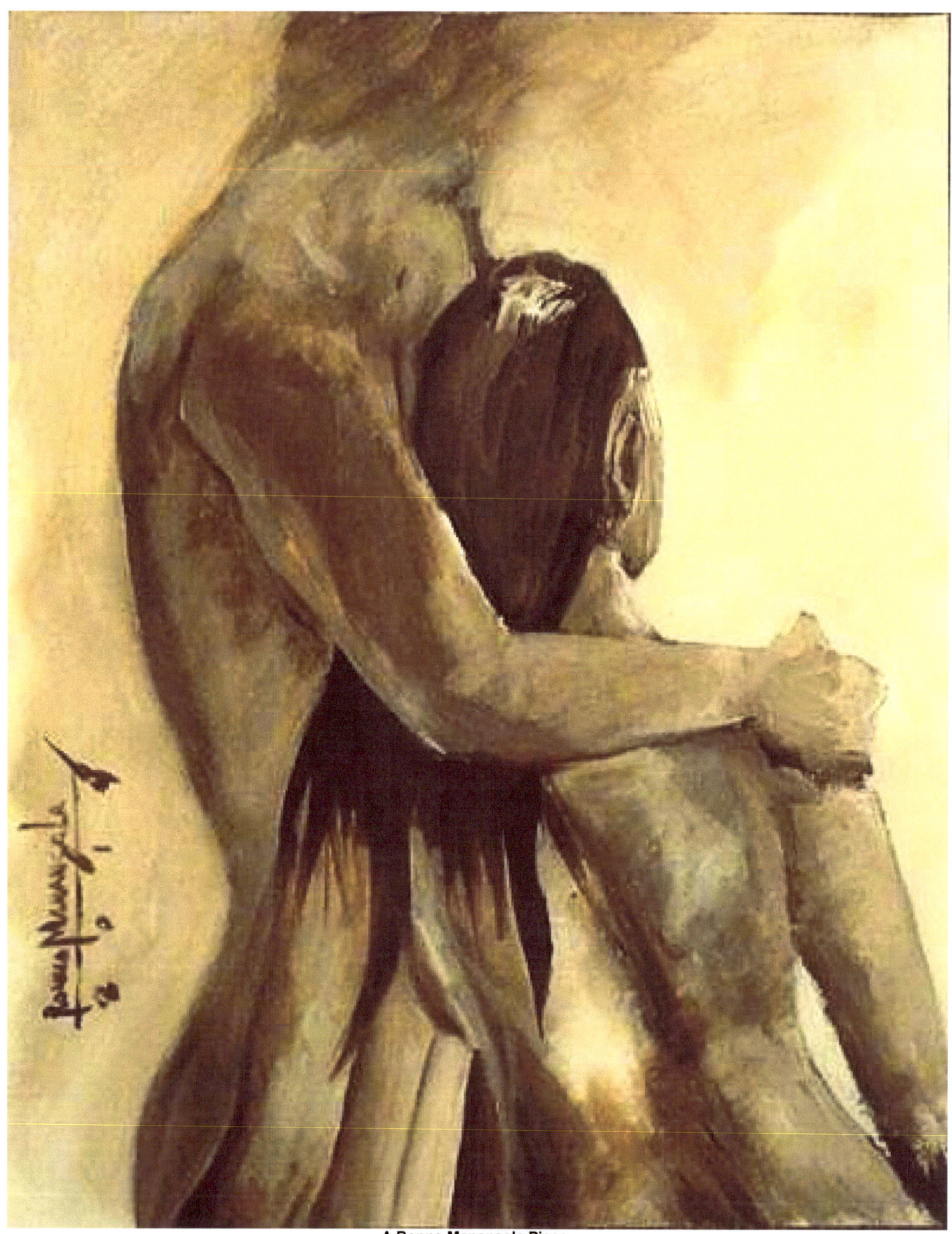

A Ronna Manansala Piece

www.ingramcontent.com/pod-product-compliance
Lightning Source LLC
Chambersburg PA
CBHW050355180526
45159CB00005B/2021